STUDENT WORKBOOK TO ACCOMPANY

REFLECT & REI

An Introduction to Interpersonal Communication

STUDENT WORKBOOK TO ACCOMPANY

REFLECT & RELATE
An Introduction to Interpersonal Communication

by Steven McCornack

Prepared by Jennifer Valencia
San Diego Miramar College

Bedford/St. Martin's
Boston ◆ New York

Manufactured in the United States of America.

1 0 9 8 7
f e d c b a

For information, write: Bedford/St. Martin's, 75 Arlington Street, Boston, MA 02116 (617-399-4000)

ISBN-10: 0-312-45910-6
ISBN-13: 978-0-312-45910-9

Preface

In the introductory interpersonal communication course there is much to learn and practice! This Student Workbook to Accompany *Reflect & Relate* is designed to help you learn the content and practice the skills covered in your textbook. Therefore, the workbook focuses on three areas: *recalling* information from your textbook, *practicing* interpersonal communication skills, and *relating* what you have learned to your life. Every chapter of the workbook contains the following elements:

- **Study Outline.** To help you learn the material in each chapter, the outline guides you through the chapter, highlighting the major points and asking you to fill in missing key terms and concepts.

- **Vocabulary Help.** I often hear that one of main challenges in studying interpersonal communication is the amount of vocabulary. To help you master key terms, each chapter contains two exercises:

  - **Word Search.** In this fun exercise, clues point to vocabulary terms hidden in the word search.

  - **Defining Key Terms.** You will be asked to explain vocabulary terms in your own words.

- **Case Study.** This activity presents you with a brief scenario about interpersonal communication and then asks five guided questions to help you critically assess the situation.

- **Self-Test.** To help you prepare for exams and check your comprehension of the chapter material, this quiz asks you twenty true or false questions. You may check your score using the Answer Key at the end of the manual, which also provides the textbook page number the question came from.

- **Journal Entry.** Critical self-reflection is an important part of applying interpersonal communication concepts to your own life; these questions prompt you to reflect on your own experiences with the material.

—Jennifer Valencia

Contents

Contents

Name: _____

Class: _____

Date: _____

STUDY OUTLINE

Fill in the blanks to complete the outline.

I. What Is Communication?

   A. The National Communication Association defines **communication** as the process through

      which people _____

      _____

      _____.

   B. There are five features that characterize communication:

      1. First, communication is a _____.

      2. Second, communicators use _____ to convey meaning.

      3. Third, communication occurs in an endless variety of situations, known as

         _____.

      4. Fourth, people communicate using various _____.

      5. And finally, communicators use a broad range of tools, known as _____.

   C. Forms of communication

      1. Communication as a field embraces a wide variety of topics.

2. Communication is a highly interdisciplinary field with collaborations in other disciplines such as _____, _____, and _____.

3. The field of communication has four broad domains:

   a. Speech and rhetorical studies deals with _____

   _____.

   b. Communication studies deals with _____

   _____.

   c. Mass communication and media studies focuses on _____

   _____.

   d. Telecommunications technologies examines _____

   _____.

4. Communication has a long history that dates back thousands of years.

   a. Communication has ancient roots.

      (1) As far back as 2200 BCE, the Egyptian Ptah Hotep wrote about enhancing

      _____.

      (2) Rhetoric comprises the _____ and _____ of

      _____ and was studied in ancient Greece and Rome by scholars

      such as Socrates and Plato who pondered the ethics of communication.

      (3) In ancient Rome, Cicero noted three goals of public speaking:

      _____, _____ , and _____.

      (4) Cicero also outlined five steps to speechmaking, which are _____,

      _____, _____, _____, and

      _____.

b. The focus of communication shifted in the early twentieth century. Two developments that set the stage for the study of interpersonal communication were

_____ and

_____ .

c. After World War II, communication became a distinct academic field for the following two reasons:

(1) _____

_____

(2) _____

_____

d. Three examples of how scholarly interest in communication intensified are:

(1) _____

_____

(2) _____

_____

(3) _____

_____

5. The primary means of acquiring trustworthy knowledge of communication is through

_____ and _____ .

a. When you conduct research you _____

_____ and then

_____ , either through

_____ or

_____ .

b. When you create a(n) _____, you create a set of descriptive statements that define your phenomenon of interest.

c. Communication scholars usually take one of two approaches in conducting research.

   (1) Qualitative approaches involve _____

   _____.

   (2) Quantitative approaches involve _____

   _____.

II. The Communication Process

   A. The **linear communication model** is the oldest.

      1. The linear model contains five components: _____,

      _____, _____, _____, and

      _____.

      2. The linear model is good for describing _____

      _____.

      3. One drawback of the linear model is _____

      _____.

   B. The **interactive communication model** builds on the first five components of the linear

      model but includes _____ and _____.

      1. The interactive model accurately describes communication such as

      _____.

      2. One drawback of the interactive model is _____

      _____.

C. The most refined model is the **transactional communication model**. The major

difference in this model is that _____

_____.

III. What Is Interpersonal Communication?

A. **Interpersonal communication** is defined as _____

_____.

B. There are four components of the definition:

1. Communication is dynamic, meaning that _____.

2. Interpersonal communication is also typically transactional but may occasionally be

_____ or _____.

3. Third, communication is **dyadic**, meaning _____.

4. Interpersonal communication changes the participants' _____,

_____, _____, and _____.

a. In perceiving relationships as **I-Thou**, we _____

_____.

b. In perceiving relationships as **I-It**, we _____

_____.

C. **Impersonal communication** has a(n) _____ on our thoughts,

emotions, behavior, and relationships.

D. Interpersonal communication actively creates _____

_____.

E. Maslow's hierarchy of needs is related to interpersonal communication because

_____

_____.

F. Three different types of goals in interpersonal communication are **self-presentation, instrumental**, and **relationship goals**.

1. Self-presentation goals are _____

_____.

2. Instrumental goals are _____

_____.

3. Relationship goals are _____

_____.

G. There are five general principles of interpersonal communication:

1. Interpersonal communication conveys both _____ and

_____.

2. Interpersonal communication can be either _____ or

_____.

3. Interpersonal communication is _____.

4. Interpersonal communication is _____.

5. Interpersonal communication is intertwined with _____.

IV. Issues in Interpersonal Communication

A. Different cultures have very different views of _____

_____.

B. Scholars disagree about how _____ influences communication.

C. Our ability to communicate easily and frequently, even when separated by geographic

distance, is further enhanced by _____.

D. Relationships, and the interpersonal communication that happens within them, are not

always joyous but can also be destructive.

V. Learning Interpersonal Communication

A. The first part of the text will demonstrate how learning about interpersonal communication

can help you _____.

B. The second part of the text is learning how to strengthen your

) _____ and master new

_____.

C. The final part of the text will illustrate how communication creates

_____, and how you can improve

communication with _____ , _____ and

_____.

WORD SEARCH

Each of the following clues describes one of the components of the models of communication. Write the term in the space provided, and then find it hidden in the word search.

1. Waving your hand, saying "Hello," or writing a note that says "Hello." _____.

2. Wearing cologne and burning scented candles while entertaining company at your home.

_____.

3. Responding to criticism with a frown, or saying "I disagree." _____.

4. A crowded room, 12:00 p.m., on a rainy day. _____.

5. Kids screaming in the background, the sun's glare, someone's strong perfume.

   _____.

6. The president when delivering a speech or your mother when she tells you to clean your room.

   _____.

7. A student being told that he/she did a good job or a worker being reprimanded for being late.

   _____.

8. The belief that running is fun, the value that hard work brings fortune, the bad attitude that all

   men are alike. _____.

```
E K U M N Z X R U W C I Y O Y B E X B P M H
O C N F T U E S I O N O W J E O A F F C E V
O W N E L V H J Y U M G N B G E G D C N S S
P O B E E U L T I R G Q I T L S H Q A Q S S
D R Q I I D V U T M Y L E H E M A A F L A E
Q M C Y D R S S U Y H D H K J X U D X D G C
U E P J S Z E X C T K G L W V X T U Z H E I
R E B R K O W P H J U K E K O O L R V V P K
J D C A C Q O R X A N O A J S J J J Y D S V K
O N O Z A P E L A E Y Z T H V P K W P D I A
X D S Q B R D H S Q F S C Z X C N P X W I E
J I O U D Q C T Y L E O P Z K W A X G R P G
L X Y I E C H A N N E L S W L W D Y F H G U
G K J L E M D X D T H Z W D Q O T B U A X L
M Q Y S F R N E G F F W T G L M E N E J W W
H B Z E O P R F Z Y L E Z O D E X P L N S P
N B Z F O K S E T D U D F Z A P I X B U Q U
K R G I Z U S W P M K U F N O N S F I R X M
I W Y S X P P O I P X V B D O S F I G A K A
W H P R K N P N L B M A U K F R M V X V P W
W Z A A I G X Z Z W M Y E M L B B A B L H L
A E M E H N M E C R Q H N M C K A Q T J L U
```

DEFINING KEY TERMS

Write a sentence that defines each of the following key terms.

1. Communication _____

_____

2. Ethics _____

_____

3. Linear communication model _____

_____

4. Interactive communication model _____

_____

5. Interpersonal communication _____

_____

6. Intrapersonal communication _____

_____

7. Impersonal communication _____

_____

8. Meta-communication _____

_____

9. Sexual orientation _____

_____

10. Interpersonal communication competence _____

_____

11. I-Thou _____

_____

12. I-It _____

_____

CASE STUDY

Read and analyze the following case study, and then answer the questions regarding the principles of communication.

Grayson, age 5, and Leila, age 2, are playing together with building blocks. Grayson is building a large fortress-like structure, while Leila is building a simple stack of blocks. Grayson has run out of blocks and says to Leila, "I need some of your blocks for my tower," while removing blocks from her stack. In response, Leila knocks over Grayson's fortress with a pout. Grayson then growls at Leila, who runs off crying.

1. According to the principles of communication, what content information is being conveyed in the scenario above?

2. How does each communicator display relationship information? What does it indicate about how they view their bond?

3. What intentional and/or unintentional message(s) could Grayson have been trying to send to Leila by growling at her?

4. What are some of the outcomes that this communication scenario might have on Grayson and Leila's relationship? If scenarios similar to this occur repeatedly, what implications might it have for their future relationship?

5. What is an example of how a similar situation might occur in an adult relationship?

SELF-TEST

For each of the following sentences, circle T if the statement is true or F if the statement is false.

T   F   1. Past communicative actions shape what you currently experience.

T   F   2. The domain of speech and rhetorical studies comprises topics such as interpersonal communication, organizational communication, and intercultural communication.

T   F   3. Mass communication and media studies examine the use, development, regulation, and impact of radio, television, telephony, the Internet, and other such technologies.

T   F   4. Ptah Hotep was an ancient Egyptian sage who wrote about interpersonal communication over 4,000 years ago.

T F 5. The three objectives of public speaking that Cicero wrote about were to instruct, to please, and to deceive.

T F 6. It wasn't until after World War II that communication studies became recognized in colleges and universities.

T F 7. The qualitative approach to writing communication theory involves testing hypothesis within carefully controlled settings.

T F 8. The linear model of communication shows information flowing in only one direction.

T F 9. The interactive model of communication suggests that transmission is influenced only by feedback and fields of experience.

T F 10. In the transactional model of communication, there aren't senders or receivers, but rather, all participants are viewed as co-communicators.

T F 11. A defining factor of interpersonal communication is that it primarily involves a dyad (two people).

T F 12. I-Thou communication means that the speaker views the other communicator as more sophisticated.

T F 13. When using I-It communication, we increase the likelihood that we'll communicate in disrespectful, manipulative, or exploitative ways.

T F 14. Interpersonal communication can help us achieve each of the levels of Maslow's hierarchy of needs.

T F 15. Meta-communication means pretending to communicate.

T F 16. Relationship outcomes can be determined by communication choices.

T F 17. Gender is determined by a person's biological sex.

T F 18. Sexual orientation refers to the two categories, homosexual and heterosexual.

T F 19. Content information includes nonverbal displays that add meaning to your words.

T F 20. Three factors that influence your communication decisions are your self, your perception of others, and your emotions.

JOURNAL ENTRY

In your last significant communication interaction (a serious talk, a meeting, an argument) with an important person in your life, what goals were you trying to pursue (self-presentation, instrumental, or relationship)? Based on what the other person communicated to you, what goals of interpersonal communication do you think he or she were trying to pursue? Give specific examples based on the verbal and nonverbal communication within the interaction.

CHAPTER 2

Considering Self

STUDY OUTLINE

Fill in the blanks to complete the outline.

I. The Components of Self

    A. The **self** is _____

        _____.

    B. **Self-awareness** is the ability to _____

        _____.

        1. **Social comparison** involves observing and assigning meaning to others' behavior and

            then _____.

        2. Critical _____ can greatly enhance your interpersonal

        communication.

    C. **Self-concept** is your overall perception of _____

        _____.

        1. Self-concept is also shaped by factors such as _____,

        _____, and _____.

        2. The impact that labeling has on our self-concepts was termed

        _____ by Charles Horton Cooley.

3. Self-concepts consist of deeply held beliefs, attitudes and values, so they are

_____ to change.

4. **Self-fulfilling prophecies** are predictions about future interactions that lead us to

behave in ways that ensure that interaction

_____.

D. **Self-esteem** is the _____.

1. **Self-discrepancy theory** suggests that your self-esteem is determined by how you

compare to two mental standards: your _____ and your

_____.

2. You can improve your self-esteem using the following five steps:

a. First, assess your _____.

b. Next, analyze your ideal self by answering the question: _____

_____?

c. Third, analyze your ought self by answering the question: _____

_____?

d. Fourth, revisit and redefine your _____.

e. Finally, create a(n) _____ by mapping out specific actions

necessary to attain your ideal and ought selves.

II. The Sources of Self

A. **Gender** is the composite of _____, _____, and

_____ that characterize us as male or female.

1. Scholars distinguish between gender, which is largely _____, and biological sex, which _____.

2. Gender is shaped through _____.

B. Our communication and interaction with family shapes our beliefs about interpersonal relationships.

1. Our _____ play a crucial role in the formation of our self-concept.

2. We adopt **attachment styles** based on the communication transactions we have with caregivers.

   a. A(n) _____ develops when a caregiver is highly affectionate and responsive during a person's infancy and early childhood.

   b. An **anxious attachment style** is formed when _____ _____.

   c. Children who grow up receiving little care or attention from any caregiver develop a(n) _____.

C. **Culture** is another powerful source of self.

1. Culture is defined as _____ _____.

2. In **individualistic cultures**, people are encouraged to focus on _____ _____.

3. In **collectivist cultures**, people are taught _____ _____.

III. Presenting Your Self

A. Others' impressions of you are based mostly on your _____.

B. Your _____ is the public self you present whenever you communicate with others.

C. We create different faces for different moments and relationships in our lives.

    1. A **mask** is a public self that you create to _____

    _____.

    2. We form a strong emotional attachment to our face because it _____

    _____.

    3. Loss of face provokes feelings of shame, humiliation, and sadness, also known as

    _____.

D. Online communication provides us with unique benefits and challenges.

    1. When communicating online, people can choose to provide clues about their public self

    by posting _____, _____, or

    _____.

    2. People communicating online can assume identities that would be _____

    _____.

    3. Three ways that we present ourselves online are through _____,

    _____, and _____.

IV. The Relational Self

A. **Social penetration theory** is the idea that we reveal ourselves to others by

_____, with the "safest"

characteristics on the outside and distinctive personality traits at the core.

    1. _____ is the number of different aspects of self each partner reveals at

    each layer.

2. _____ involves how deeply into one another's self the partners have penetrated.

B. The Johari Window has four quadrants: _____,

_____, _____, and

_____.

C. **Relational dialectics** are tensions between _____

_____.

1. Openness versus protection deals with the struggle between _____

_____.

2. In the autonomy versus connection dialectic, we struggle with conflicting desires to

_____

_____.

3. The novelty versus predictability dialectic is the clash between _____

_____.

D. The act of disclosing your self to others plays a critical role in interpersonal communication.

1. **Self-disclosure** is the act of _____

_____.

a. People vary widely in the degree to which they self-disclose.

b. People across _____ differ in their self-disclosure.

c. People disclose more _____, _____, and

_____ when interacting online than face-to-face.

d. Self-disclosure promotes _____ and relieves

_____.

e. _____ disclose more than _____, and both genders are more

willing to disclose to female than male recipients.

E. The text offers six recommendations for effectively disclosing your self:

1. Follow the advice of Apollo: _____.

2. Know _____.

3. Don't force others to _____.

4. Don't presume _____..

5. Be sensitive to _____..

6. Go _____..

WORD SEARCH

Each of the following clues describes terminology about the components of self. Write the term in the space provided, and then find it hidden in the word search.

1. A comprehensive view of the answer to the question, "Who am I?"_____.

2. "He works out every day and is so healthy. I never work out," and "She dresses so grungy every

day. I, on the other hand, like to wear designer clothes that are clean and ironed," are examples

of _____.

3. Gregory thinks he is really good at karate. He enters the dojo with confidence and is aggressive

and focused. His positive attitude contributes to an outstanding victory over a much less self-

assured opponent. Gregory goes home thinking, "I knew I would win!" This is an example of

_____.

4. William believes that others think he's a great athlete, so he formulates an image of himself in his mind as fit, agile, and exceptionally strong, even though he might be scrawny, slow, and uncoordinated. This is an example of _____.

5. The ability to step outside yourself and view yourself as a unique person distinct from your environment. _____.

6. In her mind, Corazon thinks she should be responsible and frugal. Others also expect her to be organized and punctual. This theory suggests that she might feel low self-esteem if she views herself as irresponsible, frivolous, disorganized, and always late.

    _____.

```
S L F G S T W Q U I B N Z S G Y Y R L T W Y
H O U K Z A S Q Q D M H E B F I P U A G C I
K O C B N K M A G M T L B C H N K M M E N F
U K M I T W C B R E F W P T G D X B H C R G
G I Z U A S V U Z A M N P C Y C O P Q I C D
I N H I K L Z G W B S N D X R J O P R D Z B
P G R S I V C A E V J B V W F R P F I M J P
G G O P S P R O P K Q I N S P T B E N L Z W
I L K U G E X W M E E D K G G C F Q K O H N
U A Y R N D A F D P D M N Y X K C Y P F C A
K S F E F Q A G T I A I F B H B L L G X Q N
D S S E N I P H V R L R C O A E N T F P K Z
H S M Y A E W U T L R N I N T H C X K F W A
Z E A L W C Y W I A N D A S T C N C F U H M
B L I P X C W F J T P E C N O C F L E S O I
W F N X H J L F J L L R M C U N X D H W Y H
C Z H P E U R L T O Q T M S N X S Y G B W N
L C H Y F H P A G X E C A B V E S M F J M C
Q J C F A Y K B X G D F O X D I C B B C R X
T H L G W A I A L D V H O A Q U H J D X N I
S E L F D I S C R E P A N C Y T H E O R Y M
S I C F L C D J I N R Q G T I V L I P J A B
```

DEFINING KEY TERMS

Write a sentence that defines each of the following key terms.

1. Self _____

_____

2. Self-esteem _____

_____

3. Gender _____

_____

4. Secure attachment style _____

_____

5. Anxious attachment style _____

_____

6. Culture _____

_____

7. Individualistic culture _____

_____

8. Face _____

_____

9. Mask _____

_____

10. Social penetration theory _____

_____

11. Relational dialectics _____

_____

12. Self-disclosure _____

_____

CASE STUDY

Read and analyze the following case study. Answer the questions regarding relational dialectics.

Troi and Gerry are best friends. Every Wednesday night they go out and talk about sports, work, and family life. Gerry is getting tired of this routine, but continues to go every week because he feels that he has nothing better to do. One Wednesday night, Gerry's wife, Arlene, tells Gerry that she has purchased tickets for them to see the ballet. This sounds like something new and fun to Gerry, but he hesitates to agree to go with Arlene because it means he would have to break his weekly "date" with Troi. Gerry is also slightly worried that Troi will make fun of his desire to see the ballet. When Troi calls Gerry to confirm that they will meet this Wednesday, Gerry struggles with what to tell him.

1. In what ways is Gerry struggling with telling Troi that he wants to break their weekly "date"?

2. Honesty is defined as revealing all information that is relevant to share in a situation. What information could Gerry share with Troi while still being honest? Is it possible for Gerry to tell the truth while preserving face?

3. Which of the relational dialectics (openness versus protection, autonomy versus connection, or novelty versus predictability) plays the largest role in Gerry's conflict? Explain how the dialectic is working in Gerry and Troi's relationship.

4. How do you think the struggle between relational dialectics in Gerry and Troi's relationship affect the relational dialectics in Gerry's relationship with his wife, Arlene?

5. How is the struggle between autonomy and connection different in romantic relationships versus nonromantic relationships?

SELF-TEST

For each of the following sentences, circle T if the statement is true or F if the statement is false.

T   F   1. The United States is a highly collectivist culture.

T   F   2. Your face is the self that you reveal only to your closest friends.

T   F   3. Failing to tell someone something important can be as dishonest as an outright lie.

T   F   4. When hanging out with your school friends, you pretend that you are interested in politics because you don't want to be excluded from their conversations and because you've heard them talk negatively about apolitical peers. Your efforts to appear interested in politics are known as a mask.

T   F   5. The three components of self are self-awareness, self-concept, and critical reflection.

T   F   6. Ali finds himself wanting love but unable to trust it. In relationships, he tends to be highly dependent on his significant other and always asking for a strong commitment. Ali exhibits an anxious attachment style.

T   F   7. Courtney is wearing a very loud, unattractive dress. She asks her husband, Eric, if she looks OK. He struggles with what to say because he wants to be honest, yet he doesn't want to hurt her feelings. This tension is the openness versus protection relational dialectic.

T   F   8. Gender socialization refers to the process of learning from others about what it means to be male or female.

T   F   9. The social penetration theory represents layers of information that you reveal about yourself ranging from basic facts to private feelings.

T   F   10. When dealing with online communication, it is always appropriate to disclose information.

T   F   11. Women tend to disclose more than men.

T   F   12. A good starting point for improving your self is to "know thyself."

T   F   13. Tendencies to disclose have a cultural influence.

T   F   14. You should always assume that Asian people will not disclose as much as Europeans.

T   F   15. Self-disclosure appears to promote stress and anxiety.

T   F   16. A police officer who pretends to be a 12-year-old girl online in order to catch sexual predators is wearing a mask online.

T   F   17. Everyone in Cody's family realizes he's an alcoholic, but Cody is in denial. This information is in the blind area of his Johari Window.

T   F   18. It is always ethical to disclose as long as you're being honest.

T   F   19. Gary is so spontaneous that it drives Jenn crazy! She longs for more of a daily, predictable routine. They are experiencing tension in the autonomy versus connection relational dialectic.

T   F   20. Once formed, self-esteem is impossible to improve.

JOURNAL ENTRY

What are/were the most significant factors in your life that contributed to your formation of self? How do you think gender socialization played a role in the formation of your self-concept? Who were major contributors to your self-concept? Which specific family members or caregivers had an effect on your attachment style? What role did your culture play in the formation of your self-concept?

_____

_____

_____

_____

_____

_____

_____

_____

_____

_____

_____

_____

_____

_____

_____

_____

_____

_____

CHAPTER 3

*Perceiving
Others*

Name: _____

Class: _____

Date: _____

STUDY OUTLINE

Fill in the blanks to complete the outline.

I. Perception as a Process

   A. The process of **perception** has three parts:

      1. The first step in perception is_____. In this step, we focus our

        attention on certain _____

        _____.

        a. The degree to which particular people or aspects of their communication attract our

           attention is known as _____.

      2. In **organization**, the second step, you take the information you've selected and

        _____

        _____.

        a. During organization, you engage in _____ to structure the

           information into a chronological sequence.

      3. The final step, _____, means that we

        _____.

a. We make sense of others' communication in part by comparing

_____ with

_____.

b. **Schemata** are _____

_____.

This is what we draw on when interpreting interpersonal communication.

c. As a part of interpretation, we create explanations for others' comments or behaviors.

These explanations are known as _____.

(1) _____ presume that a person's communication comes

from internal causes.

(2) _____ presume that a person's communication stems from

factors unrelated to personal qualities.

d. The **fundamental attribution error** is our tendency to attribute others' behaviors to

_____

_____.

e. The _____ is our tendency to make

external attributions regarding our own behavior.

f. We typically take credit for success by making an internal attribution known as the

_____.

g. Normally, communication stems from both _____

_____ and _____ causes.

B. Sometimes people communicate in ways we find perplexing.

    1. When we feel that we can't explain or predict someone's communication, we

    experience _____, which is especially common during

    _____.

    2. According to **Uncertainty Reduction Theory**, _____

    _____.

    3. Uncertainty can be reduced in several ways.

        a. Passive strategies for reducing uncertainty include _____

        _____.

        b. Active strategies include _____

        _____.

        c. The most direct and effective way of easing uncertainty is using _____.

II. Influences on Perception

    A. The culture in which you were raised influences your perception of others.

    1. People raised in different cultures have different knowledge in their

    _____.

    2. Your schemata are filled with _____, _____,

    _____, and _____ you learned in your own

    culture.

    3. Culture affects whether you perceive others as _____ or

    _____.

        a. **Ingroupers** are people whom you consider _____

        _____.

b. **Outgroupers** are people _____.

4. Race is judged almost entirely by _____ and affects whether we judge someone to be an _____ or an _____.

B. The relationship between gender and perception is more complicated than our stereotypes would have us believe.

1. The difference in cerebral cortex structure allows women to more accurately

    _____.

2. Canary, Emmers-Sommer, and Faulkner concluded that men and women respond in a similar manner _____ of the time when it comes to interpersonal communication.

3. People believe men and women communicate differently because _____

    _____.

C. **Personality** is another factor in how we perceive people.

1. Personality is an individual's characteristic way of _____,

    _____, and _____,

    _____.

2. The "Big Five" personality traits are _____, _____,

    _____, _____, and

    _____.

3. Our perception of others is strongly guided by _____

    _____.

4. We evaluate people positively or negatively in accordance with

    _____.

5. We presume that because a person is high or low on a certain trait that

_____.

6. _____ is the information we have about

different types of personalities and the ways in which traits cluster together.

III. Forming Impressions of Others

A. _____ are mental pictures of who people are and how we feel about

them.

B. A **Gestalt** is a _____

_____.

1. The primary advantage of Gestalts is _____

_____.

2. The primary disadvantage of Gestalts is _____

_____.

3. When Gestalts are formed, they are more likely to be positive than negative. This is

known as _____

_____.

4. The **primacy effect** is our tendency to _____

_____.

5. The **negativity effect** occurs when _____

_____.

6. The main idea behind the **halo** and **horn effects** is that _____

_____.

C. **Algebraic impressions** differ from **Gestalts** in that _____

_____.

D. One last way we form impressions is by using _____, which is a term

that describes overly simplistic interpersonal impressions.

1. One negative outcome of stereotyping is that it causes us to _____

_____.

2. Stereotyping can also create _____

_____.

IV. Improving Your Perceptions of Others

A. One of the most valuable tools for communicating more effectively with others is

_____, which we experience when we _____

_____.

1. **Perspective-taking** is _____

_____.

2. Empathetic concern encompasses _____

_____.

B. **Perception-checking** involves five steps:

1. Check your _____.

2. Check your _____.

3. Check your _____.

4. Check _____.

5. Check your _____.

WORD SEARCH

Each of the following clues is a key term from Chapter 3. Write the term in the space provided, and then find it hidden in the word search.

1. Josephine's friend Priscilla just lost her grandmother to breast cancer. Even though Josephine herself has never lost a family member to cancer, she can see why Priscilla is so sad. This is an example of showing _____.

2. Upon seeing Jacinda for the first time, Stefani sees she is well groomed, poised, and articulate. Stefani forms an all-encompassing positive first impression called a _____.

3. Because Stefani had a positive first impression of Jacinda, when Jacinda burps, Stefani thinks it's charming. This is an example of the _____ effect.

4. Rachel has been trying to quit smoking. While scanning the newspaper, a tiny advertisement in the corner for a smoking clinic jumps out at her. Her attention to the ad because of its importance to her is known as_____.

5. Khanh says that he made Desiree fall in love with him after he charmingly tripped over her dog at the park. Desiree says that she made Khanh fall in love with her after she helped him nurse his sprained ankle. Khanh and Desiree's different ways of sequencing and organizing information is an example of _____.

6. When Marcos describes his car as a low-rider, Angelica visualizes it in her mind before she sees it. The mental pattern she uses to make the information familiar is called a(n)

   _____.

7. Marci joins a stay-at-home mothers' support group and finds that she shares many similarities with them, such as an interest in scrapbooking, their family situations, and their membership in the group. She views the other mothers as _____.

8. Adolfo is quiet, shy, kind, and easy-going. These traits that guide the typical way he thinks,

feels, and acts are parts of his _____.

```
Y T V Y X P T W G Q S T Z C X W A B C M Z X
J T I U X R W X E D R C T N U E R O N T U U
G J I E R G M X O H E V U L L D U X W P Q W
R G P L M P Y P K A P N R G L H D K E I X X
R G H O A P J J V Q U J X O O S C C R E Y E
K P G Q V N A Z N A O I G S R O N A B K G O
S Z J C T K O T W O R W E W G E H F V K R K
F O G N I W R S H K G J S Z I A A S X K T R
R K F H J D Z J R Y N Y T L L Y H C G F M W
C L R R O O C M B E I J A O Y I Y X C V L L
K K V K O F S W X W P S L T Z E X P X H X W
U X N R H T F H V L Q W T U M T U G P C X R
E C G C Z U W H J W B O I W R K E M S R D L
S C H E M A T A M W P J I T B Z J B B Q Z T
M X S G Z O M A Z X T K G B O R V R A J S C
R Z M H V P P L G C F Q X L D V I I I B U X
B U B X Y U H Y X X D D J K C Z W J H G Q K
F N X Q Y R X S M P N Q M O C C B F F Q Z K
N O I T A U T C N U P H T Y W V J L K I R L
E G U P D G I R D U N E U T C D W Q G M W T
S D Y P I Y W T I Z G H O X X G C D U H I S
M D H G P Y T G S N V D E C J R C R R Y A C
```

DEFINING KEY TERMS

Write a sentence that defines each of the following key terms.

1. Fundamental attribution error _____

_____

2. Actor-observer effect _____

_____

3. Uncertainty Reduction Theory _____

_____

4. Implicit personality theories _____

_____

5. Interpersonal impressions _____

_____

6. Positivity bias _____

_____

_____

7. Primacy effect _____

_____

8. Negativity effect _____

_____

9. Self-serving bias _____

_____

10. Horn effect _____

_____

11. Algebraic impressions _____

_____

12. Perception-checking _____

_____

CASE STUDY

Read and analyze the following case study, and then answer the questions regarding how we form impressions of others.

Sam is at a picnic with his friends. There are many people Sam doesn't know at the picnic, so he strikes up a conversation with the most extroverted girl, Trang. Upon meeting Trang, Sam immediately likes her; she seems funny and smart, not to mention attractive. Trang, on the other hand, is slow to form an impression about Sam and spends much of the day observing his behavior and asking friends questions about him. She finds out he works hard as a plumber and has a large family, and she observes that he is pretty funny. So far, he seems like a good guy. As the day wears on, however, Sam starts drinking more and gets in an altercation when he loses at a game of horseshoes. At the end of the day, Sam asks Trang for her number. Trang feels conflicted because he seemed like a nice guy at first, but he then got into a fight with someone.

1. What type of Gestalt has Sam formed about Trang? What factors did he base this Gestalt upon?

2. What role did the positivity bias play in the impressions that Sam has formed of Trang?

3. What roles do the primacy effect and the negativity effect have on Trang's impression of Sam?

4. As Sam formed a Gestalt about Trang, explain how Trang developed an algebraic impression of him.

5. Do you think that Trang believes that the fact that Sam had been drinking all day and the fight he got into are related? Why or why not?

SELF-TEST

For each of the following sentences, circle T if the statement is true or F if the statement is false.

T   F   1. Algebraic impressions are formed quickly.

T   F   2. An example of the fundamental attribution error would be to assume that a coworker has often been late recently because he's lazy, not because he's been up late with his newborn baby.

T   F   3. Being empathetic means feeling sorry for someone.

T   F   4. People you consider fundamentally similar to yourself are called ingroupers.

T   F   5. When you see a cloud formation in the sky, and it resembles your old dog, you are in the organization stage of perception.

T   F   6. We tend to place extra importance on the first information we receive about a person.

T   F   7. You are more likely to notice a billboard for a debt consolidation company if you are having money problems. This is an example of high salience.

T   F   8. Shariff blames Charlotte for crashing their car, but Charlotte insists that she got in an accident because Shariff distracted her. This is an example of differences in punctuation.

T   F   9. The process of perception-checking can help you avoid errors in judgment.

T   F   10. Evita scolded the dog for having an accident in the house instead of blaming herself for forgetting to let him out all day. This is an example of the ipso-facto effect.

T   F   11. Cara is a doctor, so people assume she's smart and rich. This is an example of a stereotype.

T   F   12. When we can't predict or anticipate people's communication, we become more uncertain and tend to form negative impressions of them.

T   F   13. Personality influences our perception in terms of the traits we possess, but not how we perceive the traits of others.

T   F   14. Forming a Gestalt is the most accurate way to form an impression of someone.

T   F   15. Race is a way we classify people based on descent and is almost entirely judged by looking at physical features.

T   F   16. Everyone, regardless of race, perceives racial distinctions in the same way.

T   F   17. Due to innate differences, men and women are vastly different in their interpersonal communication styles.

T   F   18. The implicit personality theory suggests that we presume that because someone is high in one aspect (friendliness, for example), they are high in other areas (extraversion, openness) also.

T   F   19. We stereotype because it streamlines the perception process.

T   F   20. The first step in perception checking is checking your impressions.

JOURNAL ENTRY

Write about a situation where you felt as though you were classified as an outgrouper. What inaccurate stereotypes do you think the ingroupers made about you? Now, think about a time when you classified someone else as an outgrouper. Did you view them, their actions, or their communication positively or negatively? On what did you base this perception?

_____

_____

_____

_____

_____

_____

_____

_____

_____

_____

_____

_____

_____

_____

_____

_____

_____

_____

CHAPTER 4

Experiencing and Expressing Emotions

STUDY OUTLINE

Fill in the blanks to complete the outline.

I. The Nature of Emotion

    A. When we strive to translate emotions into words, we often use

    _____.

    B. Defining emotion

        1. **Emotion** is an intense reaction to an event that involves

        _____,

        _____,

        _____,

        _____, and

        _____

        _____.

        a. Emotion is reactive, which means it is triggered by _____

        _____.

        b. Emotion involves _____, in the form of increased heart

        rate, blood pressure, and adrenalin release.

c. To experience emotion, you must become _____

_____.

d. How we each experience and express our emotions is constrained by

_____, _____,

_____, and _____

_____.

e. When emotion occurs, the choices you make regarding emotion management are

reflected outward in _____ in the form of

_____.

2. Emotion is communicative in that we talk about _____

_____, a form of communication known as **emotion-sharing**.

3. **Emotional contagion** occurs when the experience of the same emotion

_____.

C. Types of emotions

1. Through examining patterns of _____,

_____, and _____, we can distinguish

among different types of emotions.

2. Scholars have identified six emotions that involve _____ and

_____ behavioral displays across cultures, known as

_____.

3. These six emotions are _____,

_____, _____,

_____, _____, and

_____.

4. A **blended emotion** occurs when _____

_____.

D. Feelings and moods

1. Emotions, feelings, and moods are not the same.

2. **Feelings** are _____

_____.

3. **Moods** are _____

_____.

a. Moods powerfully influence our perception and interpersonal communication.

b. One of the best ways to elevate your mood is through _____

_____.

II. Forces Shaping Emotion

A. Culture

1. In all cultures, **display rules** govern which forms of emotion management and

communication are _____ and _____.

2. Because of differences in _____, _____, and

_____, display rules show considerable variation across cultures.

3. Skilled interpersonal communicators adjust _____

_____ according to _____

_____.

B. Gender

1. Across cultures, women report experiencing more _____,

_____, _____, and

_____, whereas men report feeling more

_____ and _____.

2. When men and women experience the same emotion, there is no gender difference in

_____.

C. Personality

1. Three of the "Big Five" personality traits strongly influence our inward experience and

outward communication of emotion. They are _____,

_____, and _____.

2. Personality is merely one of many pieces that contribute to

_____.

III. Managing Your Emotional Experience and Expression

A. Failure to effectively manage our experience and expression of emotion can lead us to

behave in _____ ways.

1. Emotional intelligence is defined as _____

_____.

2. Emotion management involves attempts to influence

_____,

_____, and

_____.

B. Managing your emotions after they occur

   1. One strategy for managing emotions is to try to _____

     _____ after we become aware of them.

   2. **Suppression** involves _____

     _____.

   3. **Venting** is the inverse of suppression and it means to _____

     _____.

C. Preventing emotions

   1. Preventing unwanted emotions is an alternative to _____

     _____.

   2. There are four strategies for preventing emotions:

     a. **Encounter avoidance** involves _____

       _____.

     b. **Encounter structuring** is intentionally _____

       _____.

     c. **Attention focus** is devoting your attention to _____

       _____.

     d. **Deactivation** is systematically _____

       _____ to emotional experience.

D. Reappraising your emotions

   1. **Reappraisal** means actively changing _____

     _____ so that their emotional impact is changed.

2. Reappraisal is effective because you employ it before _____

_____ .

3. Reappraisal involves taking _____ for how you think about

interpersonal events.

    a. First, call to mind _____

      before _____ .

    b. Second, consider in detail _____

      _____ .

IV. Challenging Relationship Emotions

    A. Emotional experiences in close relationships are more challenging because

    _____ .

    1. **Passion** is a blended emotion that combines _____ and

    _____ .

      a. The longer and better you know someone, the less passion you will experience

        toward him or her on a daily basis because _____

        _____ .

      b. When it comes to passion, the best you can hope for in long-term romantic

        relationships is _____

        _____ .

    2. **Anger** is our most _____ and _____ emotion.

      a. Anger is a primary emotion that occurs when _____

        _____ .

b. Anger is driven largely by _____

_____.

c. The most frequently used strategy for managing anger is _____.

d. **Chronic hostility** is caused by always _____

and is a near-constant state of _____.

e. Another strategy for managing anger is _____.

(1). **Catharsis** is the concept that _____

_____.

(2) Venting provides a temporary sense of pleasure, but it actually

_____.

3. **Grief** is the intense sadness that follows _____.

a. To manage grief, you must use _____.

b. When a person uses suppression to manage grief, he or she can end up

_____

_____.

c. The best way to help others manage their grief is to engage in

_____.

V. Living a Happy and Emotional Life

A. Across all of our relationship experiences, _____ balances out our anger

and grief.

B. Through every decision we make and every thought, word, and deed, we

_____.

WORD SEARCH

Each of the following clues is a key term from Chapter 4. Write the term in the space provided, and then find it hidden in the word search.

1. When her dog died, Jordan was overcome with intense sadness. This emotion is known as

   _____.

2. Violet and Rex just started dating. When they're together, Violet feels excitement and joy, and every day they spend together is new and exciting. The blended emotion she feels is

   _____.

3. Aylin had been bothered for months by the way Sait kept interrupting her while she was talking. When Sait interrupted Aylin once again while she was telling a story, Aylin blew up at him, yelling and cursing. This explosive way of expressing emotion is known as

   _____.

4. Natalie had been attracted to Rayna since high school, but since Natalie had been taught that homosexuality was wrong, she inhibited her thoughts and displays of emotion. This is an

   example of _____.

5. Sandiq was kept up all night by his newborn baby. At his early morning meeting the next day, he was grouchy and irritable. The low-intensity state that Sandiq is in is called

   a(n) _____.

6. Isaiah is at a picnic when someone yells out that there is a swarm of bees near the playground. Soon all of the parents and picnic-goers are in a panicked frenzy to retrieve their children from the area. This rapid spreading of emotion from one person to another is called emotional

   _____.

7. Tannis is going through some old boxes when she finds her old cheerleading uniform. A wave of nostalgia and sentimentality washes over her. This short-term emotional reaction is called a(n) _____.

8. After breaking up with Darcy, Joe avoids the restaurant where they first kissed, the dry cleaner where she used to take his shirts, and the movie theater where they went every Thursday. Joe is using _____ avoidance as a strategy for preventing emotion.

```
G Z J E V G Q H J L V F T Y W L O Y C I L Z
C C T F H H J W Q I I F E N J C E K S Q D A
T D B N X A V D G M E Z O E K G J G O K K W
Q Q N I X T Q W S G L I P M L M J E Z Q C Q
X I E M M F U B S A S D Y L S I P B Z Z M L
U X Z U Q V B A R S U E Z D T R N Q Y J V H
V B V J N P A I A Z P U A E M Y M G G F B J
G M V V X O Y P Q A O G E G Q M Y L U G R X
O U W Z N I I H V T Q I B O O X D U A J X M
K Z Z W T A A G I S D U Z O D T R O G Z U Y
P P Y S Z N O F A X A L D L I K E Q F K F E
T R Y O B M R H I T H N R U U C T A V V W J
X N G F V Q T I R U N J O D D L N E S B O H
V E N T I N G O M Y L O C W V U U L D M A Q
F S B G H X Q L B R H Z C J J N O O Z N H S
N O I S S E R P P U S G Q R S I C N F Z C P
V Q U S Z Y X M O Q N R E C X M N W U M U A
H G F Z E U F I F M B I K M O G E T Z S C L
H R R J R G Y T I M D E X V B P A D O A X E
P Q Z F S X V I B H Q F F R T M I R E L Y K
H F R L R S E E F H A A N W A Z W M Q C E B
P I L M Y W H F K T K Y T K U G U P K X P F
```

DEFINING KEY TERMS

Write a sentence that defines each of the following key terms.

1. Emotion-sharing _____

_____

2. Catharsis _____

_____

3. Blended emotions _____

_____

4. Display rules _____

_____

5. Emotional intelligence _____

_____

6. Emotion management _____

_____

7. Deactivation _____

_____

8. Encounter structuring _____

_____

9. Attention focus _____

_____

10. Chronic hostility _____

_____

11. The Jefferson strategy _____

_____

12. Supportive communication _____

_____

CASE STUDY

Read and analyze the following case study, and then answer the questions regarding the nature of emotion and managing your emotional experience and expression.

Michelle has a little dog that her roommate, Lamont, does not like. One day, Lamont has a headache and the dog is barking incessantly. Lamont decides not to say anything to Michelle because he wants to avoid conflict. Instead, he just tries to concentrate on the basketball game on TV and tries to ignore the dog. The next day, after a bad day at work, Lamont comes home and discovers the dog has relieved itself on the floor. Lamont decides to leave the mess there, get back in his car, and go to a friend's house—he doesn't want to deal with the dog tonight. When Lamont gets home from his friend's house, he discovers that the dog has chewed up the controller for his video game console. Lamont gets fed up with the dog, grabs it by the scruff of the neck, and charges into Michelle's room, yelling at the top of his lungs. Naturally, a fight ensues.

1. What is the first strategy that Lamont tries to use to manage his emotions?

2. What is the second strategy that Lamont tries to use to manage his emotions? What effect does this have on the ultimate outcome of the situation?

3. How could Lamont have managed his emotions better? What strategies might he utilize the next time the dog irritates him?

4. What effect might Lamont's emotional strategies have on Michelle? What emotions might Michelle be experiencing toward Lamont?

5. How could Lamont apply the strategy of reappraisal to the described scenario?

SELF-TEST

For each of the following sentences, circle T if the statement is true or F if the statement is false.

T F 1. Emotions occur many more times a day than feelings.

T F 2. Surprise is a blended emotion.

T F 3. Display rules teach us what is culturally acceptable emotional communication.

T F 4. Catharsis is a persistent state of simmering anger.

T F 5. Gloria feels surprise and joy when she learns that she'll be a grandmother. These are examples of primary emotions.

T F 6. Grief is intense sadness that follows a substantial loss.

T F 7. The children are fighting in the back of the car, so Theo tries to concentrate even harder on the road. This is an example of attention focus.

T F 8. Teba can't stand her neighbor Trisha, so Teba never goes outside when she knows Trisha is there. This is an example of encounter structuring.

T F 9. Craig accidentally let Gerald's dog out of the house, and the dog ran away. Gerald counts to one hundred before reacting to the news. This is an example of the Jefferson strategy.

T   F   10. Carmen and Virginia are sitting in a coffeeshop talking about work. This is an example of venting.

T   F   11. Suppression is "bottling in" feelings or censoring outward displays of emotion.

T   F   12. Anger is usually triggered by someone or something we perceive as improper or unfair.

T   F   13. Laura bursts into the room with excitement; she is getting married today! This creates an excited "buzz" in the room. This is an example of emotional contagion.

T   F   14. The two most common ways people manage their emotions are through suppression and venting.

T   F   15. Reappraisal is actively changing how you think about the meaning of emotion-eliciting situations so that their emotional impact is changed.

T   F   16. Deactivating is avoiding emotion-eliciting situations.

T   F   17. Grief tends to linger for an extended amount of time compared to anger.

T   F   18. Online support groups are a viable alternative to face-to-face support groups.

T   F   19. We experience dozens, or even hundreds, of feelings daily.

T   F   20. Moods like boredom, contentment, or grouchiness are not caused by particular events.

JOURNAL ENTRY

Think of a time in your life when you experienced grief. How did you attempt to manage the grief? What strategies did others use to try to offer support or help you manage your grief? What strategies do you feel were effective? What strategies do you feel were ineffective?

_____

_____

_____

_____

_____

_____

_____

_____

_____

_____

_____

_____

_____

_____

_____

_____

_____

_____

_____

_____

Name: _____

Class: _____

Date: _____

STUDY OUTLINE

Fill in the blanks to complete the outline.

I. What Is Interpersonal Communication Competence?

   A. **Interpersonal communication competence** is communication that meets three essential

   criteria: _____, _____, and

   _____.

   B. **Appropriateness** is the degree to which _____

   _____.

   1. **High self-monitors** are people who are highly sensitive to _____

   and they _____

   _____.

   2. **Low self-monitors** believe _____

   _____.

   C. **Effectiveness** is the ability to use communication to _____

   _____.

D. The third defining characteristic of interpersonal communication competence is

_____, which means that communication decisions are

_____.

II. Crafting Competent Messages

A. Three kinds of messages

1. The goal of **expressive messages** is _____

_____.

2. **Conventional messages** emphasize _____

_____

and focus narrowly on _____.

3. **Rhetorical messages** successfully blend _____

_____.

a. Rhetorical messages address a situation's problems in a

_____ way.

b. These messages also express _____.

c. They also offer _____ to the practical problems at hand.

d. Last, rhetorical messages open doors to _____.

III. Preventing Interpersonal Incompetence

A. **Communication apprehension** is _____

_____.

B. The four types of communication apprehension are _____,

_____, _____, and _____.

1. Overcoming communication apprehension is possible by developing competent

_____, which describe _____

_____.

    a. The first element of a **communication plan** is your

    _____, or, in other words, the _____

    _____.

    b. The other element in a communication plan is your _____,

    defined as _____

    _____.

2. People who suffer communication apprehension also often experience shyness and

loneliness.

    a. **Shyness** is the tendency to be _____.

    b. **Loneliness** is defined as feelings of _____.

C. **Defensiveness** is a second type of interpersonal incompetence and consists of incompetent

messages delivered in response to _____,

_____, or _____.

    1. Four types of defensive communication are _____,

    _____, _____, and

    _____.

D. **Verbal aggression** is the tendency to _____

_____.

    1. When communicating with someone who is verbally aggressive, one should:

    a. Avoid _____.

    b. Avoid _____.

c. Remain _____.

d. End _____.

IV. Improving Your Intercultural Competence

    A. **Intercultural competence** is the ability to _____

    _____.

    B. When you possess **world-mindedness**, you demonstrate _____

    _____.

    C. The opposite of world-mindedness is _____, defined as _____

    _____.

    D. Acknowledging **attributional complexity** means recognizing that

    _____.

V. Improving Your Competence Online

    A. Understanding and adapting to online norms is the first step in developing interpersonal

    competence online.

        1. **Online disinhibition** means that people _____

        _____ during online interactions.

        2. Sending inappropriately aggressive messages that people wouldn't typically

        communicate face-to-face is known as _____.

        3. **Trolling** is an attempt to _____ by

        _____.

        4. By _____, you observe others communicating, but don't

        participate.

B. Communicating competently means knowing when to communicate online versus face-to-face.

   1. Some appropriate situations to communicate online are _____

   _____.

   2. Online communication might not be the most appropriate medium for _____

   _____.

VI. Taking Control of Competence

  A. It is the _____ that determines the

   quality of our life outcomes.

  B. You can improve the quality of your own life as well as the lives of others by

   _____.

WORD SEARCH

Each of the following clues is a key term from Chapter 5. Write the term in the space provided, and then find it hidden in the word search.

1. Connie wants to ask her boss for a raise. She visualizes and mentally rehearses the request in her mind over and over before her meeting with her boss. This is an example of a communication

   _____.

2. At an office meeting, Aunika tells Jihan, "Now that you've rambled on for 30 minutes about your idea, let me tell everyone exactly why that lame plan won't even work." This is an example of a(n) _____ message.

3. Dan tells Allen, "It doesn't matter what all the experts say. The Big Bang theory is the only explanation for how the universe was created." This is an example of a(n) _____

   message.

4. Terrance says to Indy, "When we moved in together as roommates we both agreed to take turns walking the dog. I've walked him every day this week and you haven't walked him once." This is an example of a(n) _____ message.

5. Ishmael considers doing his classroom speech on how to make a fake I.D. card. He then decides that his topic isn't principled, respectful, or honest, so he changes the topic to how to change a tire. Ishmael is practicing _____ behavior.

6. While arguing about work, Timbrel's coworker sends her an instant message calling her an "airhead who doesn't know her right from her left." This is an example of _____.

7. At a party, Radika tells several racist jokes without realizing she's offended many of the people around her. This example suggests that Radika is a(n) _____ self-monitor.

8. Rodney enters the "San Diego Chargers Fan Club" chatroom and posts several messages like "The Chargers suck!" and "The Raiders are going to dominate the Chargers on Saturday!" This is an example of _____.

```
J G Q W U A J P Z M C J Y Z T H Y C Y C T T
I T D N K T T Y P X I N C C B P O H I C M R
Y S G P H V S C N L N G N L K N L X M S H O
C O N V E N T I O N A L B G T X Z D A E A L
M T V U P K D M Z G L Q W R N F N W K E X L
Y T P H V G W O J X P F O T D I O P J Y W I
T F M I L B N W K Y W L Q N K L M G O S E N
J H P M Q K A I X Z E I S K O I L A I V T G
Y Y Y V L L U L M Y R V J I M V S Q L Q E G
N W H X Z P Z C L E V M A T H M Z D P F R P
D K X A T F Z R F M K V O L Q B I Y E R I P
F Q E D R H L C Z A L R P I I X N A C A C X
E C D F B Y F B H H J I Q C S J P Q U A K F
H D F O F T P X T Q O M Z H V Z R Y G B Q O
Z F H N I D T K G J H A B J F T N A N M U B
W W K I C M O L A C I H T E D S M B H P W C
D P M K O J O G L A R R F V A O C P Y M K T
G E N V Z T E H M R G T I K Z J I E R Q X L
A C D J T P X L L A D V K Y X X H A L Z B D
I A Y L T A O G Q Q T X N Y T X S A S W X O
Z M A O H Z M M S L C I W D O Z D Z I Y M D
K G H E K C K V M A H P C J B P W I H T X S
```

DEFINING KEY TERMS

Write a sentence that defines each of the following key terms.

1. Interpersonal communication competence _____

   _____

2. Communication skills _____

   _____

3. Expressive messages _____

   _____

4. Rhetorical messages _____

   _____

5. Communication apprehension _____

   _____

6. Defensive communication _____

   _____

7. Superiority messages _____

   _____

8. Indifference messages _____

   _____

9. Intercultural competence_____

   _____

10. Attributional complexity_____

    _____

11. Online disinhibition _____

_____

12. Lurking _____

_____

CASE STUDY

Read and analyze the following case study, and then answer the questions regarding the nature of emotion and managing your personal experience and expression.

Genevieve is a single, attractive female. She has heard a lot of positive feedback from coworkers and friends about an online dating service. She decides to give it a try. She meets a man named Jorge, and they instantly get along. Within a matter of a week, Genevieve and Jorge know so much about each other and like each other so much that they decide to meet in person. Genevieve carefully plans her outfit, washes her car, and puts on makeup. On her way to meet Jorge at her local coffeeshop, Genevieve is uncharacteristically nervous. She begins to imagine what she will say to Jorge so that he will see that she is interesting, intelligent, and funny. When they finally meet, Jorge is very quiet, almost to the point of being standoffish. Genevieve goes home, disappointed because she feels like they didn't really have any chemistry, and she is left wondering what went wrong. Jorge e-mails her later that evening and explains that he is just very nervous when talking to women and wants to try to go out with her again.

1. What role does online disinhibition play in this scenario?

2. In what ways does Genevieve use communication plans to prepare for her first meeting with Jorge?

3. From the description above, do you think Genevieve is a high self-monitor or a low self-monitor? Why?

4. What type of communication apprehension is Genevieve experiencing? What about Jorge?

5. How might Genevieve have used attributional complexity to explain Jorge's behavior?

SELF-TEST

For each of the following sentences, circle T if the statement is true or F if the statement is false.

T   F   1. Flaming is a type of incompetent communication found in online communication.

T   F   2. T.J. feels perfectly comfortable speaking to people one-on-one but is terrified of public speaking. She is experiencing trait communication apprehension.

T   F   3. Austin is the coach for the girls' volleyball team. He says to Arly, "Arly, since I am the coach, I'm letting you play on varsity, but I expect you to rise to the challenge. We're counting on you to perform up to the level of the rest of the girls." This is an example of an expressive message.

T   F   4. Interpersonal communication competence is communication that is appropriate, effective, and kind.

T   F   5. Dr. Cabalo tells Sameena that her speech could have been better with a few more transitions. Sameena responds by saying, "Well, transitions aren't that important. Who listens to the transitions, anyway?" This response is an example of defensive communication.

T   F   6. Farley behaves the same way in every situation, not bothering to alter his communication or abide by norms. He is considered a high self-monitor.

T   F   7. Routinely checking your perceptions of others is a method for avoiding making attributional errors.

T   F   8. Damien is the highest-grossing sales agent at his firm. Since he is appropriate and effective, this means he is a competent communicator, regardless of the fact that he sometimes uses unethical methods to sell the products.

T   F   9. Learning communication skills is the first step in developing interpersonal communication competence.

T   F   10. Before Angela has a big job interview, she mentally rehearses what she will say and anticipates questions she will be asked. This is an example of a communication plan.

T   F   11. When Maria visits the Philippines, she just can't understand why the people eat with their hands. It seems so rude and unsanitary! This is an example of ethnocentrism.

T   F   12. People lurking in online chatrooms are looking for opportunities to commit crime or fraud.

T   F   13. There are four types of communication apprehension: context, receiver, sender, and trust.

T   F   14. People who always believe they are right, and the other party is wrong, will often use dogmatic messages.

T   F   15. Competent interpersonal communication must meet three criteria: it must be principled, respectful, and honest.

T   F   16. Disclosing personal thoughts or messages in the form of expressive messages is considered effective and appropriate communication.

T   F   17. Saying "Your opinion doesn't really matter, so I made the decision without you" is an example of an indifference message.

T   F   18. Cynthia is late for a meeting at work. Before she enters the meeting, she mentally anticipates the different ways that her coworkers will react and thinks of ways she might respond. This is an example of a plan contingency.

T   F   19. When posting her profile on an online dating service Web site, Andrea finds herself revealing much more personal information than she would in person. This is an example of online disinhibition.

T   F   20. After living in different parts of Mexico for several months, Laura has gained an appreciation and respect for Mexican beliefs, customs, and traditions. This is an example of world-mindedness.

JOURNAL ENTRY

Do you consider yourself to be a high or a low self-monitor? Why? Cite specific examples in your behavior and communication style in different contexts (work, school, home, and so on.). Do you believe that your self-monitoring style helps or hinders your interpersonal communication? Why?

_____

_____

_____

_____

_____

_____

_____

_____

_____

_____

_____

_____

_____

_____

_____

_____

_____

_____

Name: _____

Class: _____

Date: _____

STUDY OUTLINE

Fill in the blanks to complete the outline.

I. Basics of Listening

    A. **Listening** is our most _____ and _____ skill.

    B. We have the potential to develop our listening into something more

    _____ than passive "down time" while others are speaking.

II. Listening: A Five-Step Process

    A. Receiving

        1. Together, _____ and _____ constitute **receiving**.

        2. You can enhance your ability to receive and listen by becoming aware of

        _____.

    B. Attending

        1. **Attending** involves _____ to the information you've received.

        2. The extent to which you attend to received information is largely determined by its

        _____.

3. You can engage in _____ when your attention wanders, by

_____

_____.

C. Understanding

1. **Understanding** involves _____ by

comparing _____

_____.

2. **Short-term memory** is where you place _____

_____.

3. **Long-term memory** is the part of your mind devoted to _____.

D. Responding

1. **Responding** is communicating _____ and _____.

2. **Feedback** is verbal and nonverbal behaviors used to communicate understanding and

attention while _____.

a. _____ is one type of feedback.

b. To effectively display positive feedback, you should make your feedback

_____, _____, _____, and

_____.

3. Active listeners communicate attention and understanding after the other person is done

speaking.

a. **Paraphrasing** is _____.

b. You should couple your paraphrasing with _____

_____.

E. Recalling

    1. **Recalling** is _____.

    2. Recall is only as accurate as your _____.

    3. Recall accuracy also depends on the _____.

    4. You can improve your recall ability by using _____ and

    _____.

III.   Why Listen: Five Purposes

    A. Listening to comprehend means that you work to _____

    _____ the information that you receive.

    B. Listening to support is providing _____ to a conversational partner.

    C. When listening to analyze, you carefully evaluate the message you're receiving and you

    _____.

    D. When listening to appreciate, your goal is simply to _____

    _____.

    E. Listening to discern means focusing on _____

    _____.

    F. The five **listening functions** are not mutually _____.

IV.   Understanding Listening Styles

    A. A **listening style** is your habitual pattern of listening behaviors, which reflects

    _____, _____, and _____.

    1. **Action-oriented** listeners want _____

    _____.

2. **Time-oriented** listeners prefer _____ encounters.

3. **People-oriented** listeners view listening as _____

_____.

4. **Content-oriented** listeners prefer to be _____

_____.

B. Women and men consistently differ in their preferences for and practices of

_____.

1. Women are more likely to use _____ and

_____ listening styles.

2. Men tend to use _____ and _____ listening

styles.

C. What is considered effective listening by one culture is often perceived as

_____ by others.

1. _____ and _____ listening styles are dominant in

individualistic cultures, such as _____.

2. _____ and _____ listening styles are more

common in collectivist cultures, such as _____.

V. Preventing Ineffective Listening

A. **Selective listening** means taking in only _____ during an

interpersonal encounter and _____.

B. **Eavesdropping** occurs when people intentionally and systematically

_____.

C. **Pseudo-listening** means behaving _____

_____.

D. **Aggressive listening** is attending to what others say solely to _____

_____.

E. **Narcissistic listening** is self-absorbed listening where the person ignores what others have

to say and _____.

VI. The Gift of Active Listening

A. Listening poses many challenges for us when we reach adulthood.

B. We struggle with listening in part because it's exceptionally demanding.

C. We can surmount the challenges of active listening by _____,

_____, _____, and _____.

WORD SEARCH

Each of the following clues is a key term from Chapter 6. Write the term in the space provided, and then find it hidden in the word search.

1. Lorelei is watching the news and waiting for the traffic report. When it comes on, she

   consciously focuses her attention on the television. This is an example of_____.

2. Kaveh's mother tells him to stand up straight and tuck in his shirt. In response to this, Kaveh

   rolls his eyes. His response is an example of _____.

3. Miguel remembers the names of all of his grandchildren. This information is stored in his

   _____ memory.

4. The prefixes in the metric system can be remembered using the following saying: King Henry

   Died Monday Drinking Chocolate Milk (Kilo-, Hecto-, Deca-, Main unit, Deci-, Centi-, Milli-).

   This is an example of a(n) _____.

5. Darren told his girlfriend, Bituin, that he was listening to her but he was actually checking his e-mail. This is a form of _____ listening.

6. Tang asks Donella to tell her all about Donella's family trip to Europe because she enjoys hearing about Donella's experiences with the food, culture, and art. Tang is a _____-oriented listener.

7. Kim repeated his number several times, but Autumn just couldn't remember it. Autumn is experiencing difficulty with the _____ stage of the listening process.

8. Yumiko's mother asks her to do three things: put the laundry in the dryer, start the dishwasher, and pick up a chocolate cake for dessert. Yumiko listens and responds only to the message about chocolate cake because it's her favorite food. This is an example of _____ listening.

```
X D F V R L Y T G L Q F E D Q I K L W M E P
I D Z N R B T N Y M E M Z T C N I V I T L R
U M J C E B I W C E Y M L E Q I Z Q T T P K
G M B D L D Z R D R I D L R S X N W D S O V
M T B O N X U B E M R E T G N O L O E E E W
M Y C E C C A M R C A M X X Z X H F M L P B
X S T U Z C L E I X A G K B N F J W L E M M
U T Z J K T R V S K D L K K L V B J A C N W
A V N G M K B F Z Z F F L A A V H A P T T M
A V L U M S Z Q P P X M O I L O F Q Z I B P
D R H Z W Z J E J Q F I W N N P K G O V A T
J W K Y K J K S V G R L G D R G T V E E F D
S P D H U E D F S O V Y F C I J O O S E J R
B J O E K Q S A K L L T Q U J F U W X Q Q I
S R L K C Y S T V R Y X D U V V Y Y R R O B
Z Z C B J Z W S S C J A O T A K S Q S R D U
Y V E L D H V N K L B M B Q H O R K J S M L
A J W Z X N A L R C F T Q U N Q Q Z S I D D
Q K K D L X H I O W X D F U U W F P E O V V
P L A X S J V X J N G K Z N X P B Q O Q B K
J L L E O K Z J P R L P E J I G T M X E G M
A M B U S H I N G R U Z R V H Z N C E G F Y
```

DEFINING KEY TERMS

Write a sentence that defines each of the following key terms.

1. Mental bracketing _____

_____

2. Short-term memory _____

_____

3. Back-channel cues _____

_____

4. Bizarreness effect _____

_____

5. Listening functions _____

_____

6. Action-oriented listeners _____

_____

7. Time-oriented listeners _____

_____

8. Provocateurs _____

_____

9. Content-oriented listeners _____

_____

10. Selective listening _____

_____

11. Aggressive listening _____

_____

12. Narcissistic listening _____

_____

CASE STUDY

Read and analyze the following case study, and then answer the questions regarding active listening.

Thirteen-year-old Isabella is unhappy because a boy she likes at school doesn't seem to notice her. Isabella's mother, Leigh, notices that Isabella is upset and asks her what's wrong. Isabella explains the situation. Leigh immediately responds that Isabella is much too young to be interested in boys and that fraternizing with the opposite gender is inappropriate. This just makes Isabella more upset, and she says that Leigh never listens to her. Leigh immediately begins giving Isabella advice on love and relationships. Isabella sighs and nods, pretending to listen, even though she doesn't really want the advice.

1. At the beginning of the scenario, what type of listening is Leigh exemplifying?

2. Why does Leigh's initial response upset Isabella even further?

3. If Leigh listens to analyze with Isabella, what is likely to happen in future communication interactions between them?

4. Why doesn't Isabella want to hear the relationship advice? What type of listening would be most effective in this scenario?

5. What type of ineffective listening behavior does Isabella exhibit?

SELF-TEST

For each of the following sentences, circle T if the statement is true or F if the statement is false.

T   F   1. Employees at fast-food restaurants often use an action-oriented listening style.

T   F   2. When a lawyer cross-examines a witness and is looking for discrepancies in his or her testimony, the lawyer is engaged in aggressive listening.

T   F   3. Hearing is the same as attending.

T   F   4. Giving a "thumbs up" signal after your boss asks you how it's going is an example of a back-channel cue.

T   F   5. We are less likely to remember information if it is odd or unusual.

T F 6. Content-oriented listeners prefer to hear messages with a lot of emotional connections.

T F 7. Eavesdropping can occur accidentally.

T F 8. Thelma gives Gene flowers with a message that says, "Thinking of you." Gene responds by giving her a warm embrace. The embrace is an example of feedback.

T F 9. Hearing and listening are the same thing.

T F 10. Listening to a comedy show is an example of listening to discern.

T F 11. Memories of your first trip to Disneyland at age 6 would be stored in your long-term memory.

T F 12. Mental bracketing leads to ineffective listening.

T F 13. "My Very Educated Mother Just Served Us Nine Pizzas" is an example of a mnemonic device used to remember the planets in our solar system.

T F 14. When talking with her friends, Heidi keeps changing the topic so that she is the center of the conversation. This is an example of narcissistic listening.

T F 15. Every day, Melissa asks her son Adam what he did in school that day. Melissa believes this habit strengthens her relationship with her son. In this example, Melissa is a people-oriented listener.

T F 16. Provocateurs enjoy encouraging others to share emotional experiences in online chatrooms.

T F 17. If you've forgotten where you left your mobile phone, you've had a lapse in your short-term memory.

T F 18. Professor Knight told her student Lily, "What's your question? And make it quick— my office hours end in five minutes." This is an example of a time-oriented listener.

T F 19. James's dad says, "Son, after you clean your room and eat lunch, you can have some ice cream." All James focuses on is the part where his dad mentions "ice cream." This is the recalling stage of the listening process.

T F 20. Seeing is a sensory process that is essential to the receiving step of the listening process.

JOURNAL ENTRY

Describe a time when someone practiced ineffective listening behavior while you were trying to communicate with him or her. Define the ineffective listening method he or she used. How did you react? Did it cause a conflict to occur? How did this occurrence affect your relationship with the other party?

_____

_____

_____

_____

_____

_____

_____

_____

_____

_____

_____

_____

_____

_____

_____

_____

_____

_____

_____

_____

CHAPTER 7

Communicating Verbally

STUDY OUTLINE

Fill in the blanks to complete the outline.

I. Characteristics of Verbal Communication

  A. **Verbal communication** is the exchange of _____

    _____.

  B. Language has five fundamental characteristics:

    1. Language is basically a giant collection of _____ in the form of words

      that allow us to communicate; therefore, language is _____.

    2. Language is governed by _____.

      a. _____ rules tell us which words represent which objects.

      b. _____ rules represent the do's and don'ts and guide everything

        from _____ to _____ to

        _____.

  C. Language is flexible.

    1. Personal idioms are words and phrases that have _____ within

      _____.

2. When large groups of people share creative variations on language rules, those

variations are called _____.

3. Language is cultural in that it is the _____ that members of a

culture create to communicate their _____.

D. **Low-context cultures** tailor their verbal communication to be _____

_____.

1. In **high-context cultures** people don't feel a need to provide a lot of

_____ to gain a listener's understanding.

2. Language evolves; it is constantly _____. People add new words

and phrases to their language and discard old ones. A language's

_____ also change.

II. Functions of Verbal Communication

A. Verbal communication enables us to share _____ with others

during _____.

1. _____ is the literal meaning of words, agreed upon by members

of a culture.

2. _____ is a word's additional understandings based on the

situation and the knowledge we and our communication partners have.

B. Verbal communication shapes our _____

_____.

1. The belief that language defines the boundaries of our thinking is

known as _____.

2. The idea that people from different cultures would perceive and think about the world in

very different ways because language determines thought is known as _____.

C. **Naming** is creating _____ for objects.

D. Verbal communication enables us to perform _____, known as

_____.

   1. The five types of **speech acts** are _____,

_____, _____,

_____, and _____.

E. Language happens within _____.

   1. Conversations are _____ in that at least two people must

participate in talk exchange.

   2. Conversations are _____ managed, and the people having the

conversation decide _____, _____,

_____, and _____.

   3. Conversation is universal. Conversation forms the foundation for _____

_____.

F. To forge, maintain, and end _____ is the most profound purpose of

verbal communication.

III. Cooperative Verbal Communication

   A. **Cooperative verbal communication** means that you produce messages that

_____, that

_____, and that others feel

_____.

B. Paul Grice's _____ argues that meaningful interactions rest on our ability to tailor our verbal communication in certain ways so that others can understand us.

1. Being informative means presenting _____ but not disclosing information that isn't _____.

2. People count on the fact that the information that you share with them is _____, so you should be _____.

3. Being relevant means making your conversational contributions _____.

4. Be clear by presenting information in a _____, not in ambiguous terms.

5. Using **"I" language** means that you use phrases that emphasize _____ for your _____, _____, and _____.

6. Wordings that emphasize inclusion are known as _____.

C. When it comes to men's and women's verbal communication styles, research suggests that _____ _____.

D. Culture exerts _____ on verbal communication.

1. **Communication accommodation theory** states that people are more motivated to _____ when they _____.

2. Research suggests that when you _____ adjust your language use to match that of others from different cultures, you will be perceived as _____.

IV. Barriers to Cooperative Verbal Communication

    A. **Mispresentation** is, simply put, _____.

        1. Intentional mispresentation is called _____.

        2. When someone intentionally mispresents information it isn't always out of

        _____ intent.

    B. **Misunderstanding** occurs when one person misperceives another's thoughts, feelings, or

        beliefs as expressed in the other individual's _____ .

        1. Failure to _____ is the first cause of misunderstanding.

        2. _____ is another, albeit strange, cause of unintentional

        misunderstanding.

        3. The third cause of unintentional misunderstanding is when people innocently

        _____.

        4. Misunderstanding can happen unintentionally or _____.

V. The Power of Verbal Communication

    A. The power of language is experienced as intensely _____.

    B. The words we exchange profoundly affect not only our interpersonal communication and

        relationships but also _____.

WORD SEARCH

Each of the following clues is a key term from Chapter 7. Write the term in the space provided, and then find it hidden in the word search.

1. While selling Mary a used car, Jesse omitted the fact that the car had been in a flood and three

    accidents. Intentionally omitting these important details is an example of _____.

2. William tells the Girl Scout who comes to his door selling cookies, "Sorry, I would buy some but I don't have any money." This direct and clear manner of speaking is characteristic of _____ cultures.

3. Manolo and Hailee call each other "love bug." This is an example of a personal _____.

4. Christina asks Marie, "Have you eaten dinner yet?" and Marie responds, "No. What do you feel like tonight?" These discrete units of conversation are known as _____.

5. Naveen tells the engineering team, "You guys just can't seem to pull it together before the deadline! You need to concentrate and stop messing around!" This accusatory style of communication is called _____ language.

6. The word *can* has several meanings: it is a metal vessel for storing food, it refers to the ability to do something, and it is also slang for getting terminated from a job. These are all _____ meanings.

7. Julia told Roy to pick her up outside the bar. Roy waited outside the side entrance to the bar, while Julia was out front. This is an example of a(n) _____.

8. In Roman numerals, *I* represents "one," *II* represents "two," and so forth. Roman numerals are an example of _____.

```
L M A D S J M L U H M O E V W O G Z R S E E
F U D E F B M P M W T G M D E I O P C X A U
E A T N F N A S T L K G Q T A D A X E B D C
C A H P W X G R V X I N E I R U S V J X I T
M I S U N D E R S T A N D I N G P I D S T C
L Q U X W C J F V D W K P N L A E D C K E L
Z O P L K U E A E F L K V I P M E G H F M V
B O W U G F F N Q O C O Y T E K C L P X U X
M M H C V X O H G D R C N J A Z H H A K D H
A U C C O T P H S I W K S R E V A V N C M L
A V E B A N H Z Y L L L T F X G C Z S I Q L
Z U T T R P T I D R O M A F F N T B X I L S
Y H I R U U B E U N O B X Q Z K S U H K B E
A V R D Q C M X X E F J M Y F V I Q R F K C
E E C T K T G R T T R W E Y K M I H U H W D
F L N L V A M I Z J D O U O S O F V Y R K S
A H G M Z W F Q U Z W C H B S I H R F V W Q
L X I H U X V B Y T Z P M T G D F S V Y R C
X H B O R D Z H I F W O C D Z I H W S T R W
S J Y L Z G N O I T P E C E D C H N S W D X
V A G W L Z F V G K M Q Z B G I A B H R P H
T Z E P G Q T I B B X Q F X R X S K N J O D
```

DEFINING KEY TERMS

Write a sentence that defines each of the following key terms.

1. High-context cultures _____

   _____

2. Connotative meanings_____

   _____

3. Linguistic determinism _____

   _____

4. Linguistic relativity_____

   _____

5. Cooperative verbal communication _____

_____

6. Cooperative Principle _____

_____

7. Communication accommodation theory _____

_____

8. "I" language _____

_____

9. Naming _____

_____

10. Dialects _____

_____

11. Constitutive rules _____

_____

12. Regulative rules _____

_____

CASE STUDY

Read and analyze the following case study, and then answer the questions regarding cooperative verbal communication and mispresentation.

Ashley and Arthur have been dating for two years. Last night as Arthur was walking out the door, he told Ashley, "I'll be back!" and waved over his shoulder. Now it's 7:30 a.m. and Ashley has been waiting up all night. Arthur finally walks in the front door with a nonchalant expression on his face. He smiles and greets Ashley with, "Good morning. You're up early." After seeing that he's not injured, Ashley exclaims, "Geez, Arthur! You didn't even call me! Where have you been? You inconsiderate jerk!" Arthur's facial expression changes immediately. He yells back, "It's none of your business where I've been! You're not my mother! I don't always have to report to you!" Ashley takes a deep breath and collects herself. She replies, "I was worried sick when you didn't call or come home. I called every hospital just to be sure you hadn't gotten into an accident." Arthur is still fuming. "Nobody asked you to look after me!" he yells. Ashley doesn't want to engage in further conflict, so she tells Arthur she's going for a walk. When she comes home two hours later, ready to talk it out, she finds a note from Arthur that simply reads, "I need some time away. I'm sorry." Ashley is sad and confused.

1. How is Arthur's message of "I'll be back!" an example of poor cooperative verbal communication?

2. What are some examples of "you" language in this scenario?

3. How does the use of "you" language escalate the conflict?

4. How is "I" language used in the scenario?

5. Do you think the cause of this argument is a misunderstanding, a misrepresentation, or something else?

SELF-TEST

For each of the following sentences, circle T if the statement is true or F if the statement is false.

T F 1. An engagement ring is a symbol.

T F 2. Kevin tells his girlfriend, "We need to be better at managing our finances." This is an example of a speech act.

T F 3. The term *verbal communication* refers only spoken language, not to written communication.

T F 4. Kurt is talking to his new boss, Tony, for the first time. Kurt adjusts his speech rate and clarity to match Tony's. This helps make a favorable impression. This is an example of the Constitutive Principle.

T F 5. The connotative meaning of a word is the dictionary definition or literal meaning.

T F 6. Cooperative verbal communication means speaking in a clear, inclusive, and responsible way.

T F 7. If you omit important details on purpose, you are being deceptive.

T F 8. "Beating around the bush" and saying things in an indirect manner are characteristics of high-contexts cultures.

T F 9. "I waited for over an hour, and you didn't even bother to call to tell me you were going to be late!" said Tabitha. This is an example of "I" language.

T F 10. There are several different words for "waves" in Hawaiian, but in English, we only have one; therefore, English speakers have a limited way of perceiving waves compared to Hawaiian speakers. This is an example of linguistic relativity.

T F 11. Misrepresentations can occur intentionally or unintentionally.

T F 12. When Jade was a baby she used to make grunting and growling noises like a bear, so now, even as a teenager, her family members still call her Bear. This is an example of a personal idiom.

T F 13. The idea that we talk one at a time as opposed to everyone talking at once is an example of a regulative rule.

T F 14. One characteristic of language is that its constitutive rules may change but its regulative rules are constant.

T F 15. Raul left a note on the refrigerator for Mona that read, "I left a slice of pie for you. Have a good day!" The note is an example of verbal communication.

T F 16. Annabelle is presenting a speech in front of the city council. She accidentally reports inaccurate statistics about the crime rate. This is an example of a mispresentation.

T F 17. "I" language is the opposite of "we" language.

T F 18. In Tagalog, the national language of the Philippines, *mahal* means both "love" and "expensive." This is an example of a dialect.

T F 19. Even though people all over the world speak different languages, we all tend to perceive the world in a similar way.

T F 20. Misunderstandings are always unintentional.

JOURNAL ENTRY

Write about a time where you experienced a misunderstanding. What was the cause of the misunderstanding (poor listening, relationship intimacy, misinterpretation)? What effects did it have on the situation or the relationship? Did it escalate into an argument? What can be done within the relationship to avoid misunderstanding in the same context in the future?

_____

_____

_____

_____

_____

_____

_____

_____

_____

_____

_____

_____

_____

_____

_____

_____

_____

_____

CHAPTER 8
Communicating Nonverbally

STUDY OUTLINE

Fill in the blanks to complete the outline.

I. Principles of Nonverbal Communication

    A. **Nonverbal communication** is the intentional or unintentional transmission of meaning

        through _____

        _____.

        1. Nonverbal communication uses multiple _____, including

           _____, and _____.

        2. Nonverbal meanings are more _____ and _____.

        3. Nonverbal communication is governed by fewer _____.

        4. Nonverbal communication has more _____; actions speak louder

        than words.

        5. Nonverbal and verbal combine to create _____.

    B. Nonverbal communication and gender

        1. People possess _____ about how the different genders use

        nonverbal communication and what men and women consider appropriate nonverbal

        expression.

2. Research on nonverbal communication _____ some of these beliefs.

    a. Women are better than men at both _____ and

       _____ nonverbal messages.

    b. Women show greater facial _____ than men.

    c. Women _____ at others more during interpersonal interactions.

    d. Men maintain more physical _____ during encounters.

C. Nonverbal communication and culture are _____ linked.

    1. The link between culture and nonverbal communication makes cross-cultural

      communication _____.

    2. Most people need _____

      _____ before they fully understand the meanings of that culture's

  nonverbal communication.

II. Nonverbal Communication Codes

  A. _____ is the study of communicating through body movements, such as

  facial expression, eye contact, gestures, and body postures.

    1. The shifting in facial expressions based on one's viewing perspective is known as

      _____.

    2. We can use _____ to express emotions or convey hostility.

    3. The category of gestures known as **emblems** represent _____

      _____. Whereas _____

  accent or illustrate verbal messages.

    4. **Regulators** control _____ , whereas **adaptors**

      are touching gestures that _____.

5. **Posture** communicates both _____ and _____.

B. **Vocalics** are vocal _____ we use to communicate nonverbal

messages and include _____, _____,

_____, and _____.

C. Communicating through touch is known as _____.

1. Scholars distinguish between five types of touch: _____,

_____, _____,

_____, and _____.

D. Communicating through personal space is called _____.

1. Intimate space ranges from _____ to _____.

2. _____ ranges between 18 inches to 4 feet.

3. Social distance ranges between _____.

4. _____ ranges from 12 feet or more.

E. The way you use time to communicate during interpersonal encounters is called

_____.

1. People who have **M-time** orientation value _____

_____.

2. People who have **P-time** orientation value _____

_____.

F. How you look conveys as much about you as what you say because we communicate

through _____.

G. _____ are the things we possess that influence how we see ourselves and

that we use to express our identity to others.

H. We communicate through our **environment**, the _____ of our surroundings

with _____ features and _____ features.

III. Functions of Nonverbal Communication

A. We sometimes use nonverbal communication to _____ convey

_____, like giving a thumbs-up to indicate a good job.

B. We use nonverbal communication more indirectly in five ways:

1. To _____ verbal messages, such as pointing left and saying "Turn left

here."

2. To _____ our verbal messages, such as saying we're not angry when

we're scowling.

3. To _____ the meaning of verbal messages, such as holding a scared

child close while telling him that he's safe.

4. To _____ verbal expressions altogether, such as simply nodding to

communicate agreement.

5. To _____ certain parts of messages, such as saying one word more

loudly than others: "STOP running by the pool."

C. Nonverbal communication in the form of _____ can be used to

intentionally or unintentionally to communicate emotion.

D. Nonverbal communication can help us present different _____

_____ to others.

E. Nonverbal communication helps us _____ interpersonal interactions.

F. We also use our nonverbal communication to create _____ and to define

_____ or _____ in our relationships.

1. Nonverbal communication helps to create **intimacy**, which is a feeling of

_____

_____.

2. Nonverbal communication can also convey **dominance** and _____.

IV. Responsibly Managing Your Nonverbal Communication

A. In interactions, you use various nonverbal communication codes naturally and

_____.

B. Nonverbal communication often speaks _____ than verbal communication.

C. Nonverbal communication effectiveness is inextricably tied to _____.

D. Be sensitive to the demands of interpersonal situations and adapt your nonverbal

communication _____.

E. A skilled interpersonal communicator focuses on both _____ and

_____ communication.

WORD SEARCH

Each of the following clues is a key term from Chapter 8. Write the term in the space provided, and then find it hidden in the word search.

1. Domingo drives a Mercedes, wears designer suits, and owns the biggest house on the block.

These objects that he uses to influence how others view him are called _____.

2. Thomas is driving down the freeway when another driver cuts him off. Thomas rolls down his

window and brandishes a fist at the other driver. This gesture that symbolizes anger is known as

a(n) _____.

3. When Jeff starts talking, Rachelle sits up straight, stops what she is doing, and looks at him. The

interest that Rachelle conveys through her body language is called _____.

4. Hienzel answers the telephone at work, "Financial Fitness Incorporated. I'll be happy to help you," with a bored, uninviting tone. This contradiction between her verbal and nonverbal communication is an example of a(n) _____ message.

5. Lani and the rest of her family decide that it's all right to be a little late to their cousin's party because they are enjoying the sun at the beach so much. This cultural orientation towards viewing time loosely is called _____.

6. Increasing your volume when speaking might signal anger or surprise, or might help the other person hear more clearly. The nonverbal code that represents vocal characteristics is known as _____.

7. Solon holds her patient's arm while giving him a flu shot. This type of touch is known as _____-professional touch.

8. Nati and Tanisha are talking excitedly at a busy coffeeshop about Tanisha's date that night. The proxemic zone that they are most likely inhabiting is known as _____ space.

```
M D U K M O K D V V W F D S U M P C M Q Z H
S X A W D U H L P Z E U U R C K B E X K P R
Q T D R B M G Q O D W N B P O I L J U Y H G
C G W I Y X P J L W P C U W T B L P R E E G
Y P K V K S R N D N P T W G M I C A L X K A
R N T N W C B S D E M I V E W R M B C F P C
Y A Y C A I D E M M I O B I O A L E N O R F
D R D S L N G H X N N N U M R A A U R A V U
K J N A B T S O E F E A B T Z Y N S L Y Y L
O X K J B M P B E V R L I P R K O X J H X S
K F O X N X R E C H K F R Y Y R S Z N W Q N
B Z Y R P Q S U N N A J X W O E R C T O K Y
Y J J B Q D J G X C B V P U B Y E C J T O F
I G F H J O E Q T P D X J V K P P G U X C W
U P H A N E J S I C D R F L N N W W H O X T
Y A T W A P P O K J R H L Y N O J W Q Z J M
I N G U Z D X P J P U D G P T O L B W B Q Q
W Z C R R I F D Z K H D K V V J W T T V T E
G F C V N Z H A Z A M V N L C R L T M W Z B
D R S R T K X M I X E D C W B Z W Q V S A T
D Z P U X P Q Q V N Z L G B V J C Y H B Z O
B D R T S W Z S T G J Z N H O A U K Q T Y I
```

DEFINING KEY TERMS

Write a sentence that defines each of the following key terms.

1. Nonverbal communication _____

_____

2. Nonverbal communication codes _____

_____

3. Power _____

_____

4. Social-polite touch _____

_____

5. Proxemics _____

_____

6. Territoriality _____

_____

7. M-time _____

_____

8. Intimate space _____

_____

9. Physical appearance _____

_____

10. Affect displays _____

_____

11. Dominance _____

_____

12. Submissiveness _____

_____

CASE STUDY

Read and analyze the following case study, and then answer the questions regarding nonverbal communication.

Max and Tito are at the mall sitting in front of the arcade. They are talking about nothing of consequence when Max notices a group of boys standing a few yards away who keep looking at them, whispering to each other, and then laughing. Max and Tito make eye contact and Max nods his head toward the group of boys. Tito looks over and sees the group staring and laughing. Tito stares back at the group with a menacing scowl. One boy in the group turns around and points to a patch on his jacket that reads, "Tae Kwon Do Champion 2006" on it. Max and Tito look at the patch and look at each other, and both sarcastically chew their fingernails as if to mock the other boy. Then Max and Tito fall into a fit of laughter. The boy wearing the patch cracks his knuckles, and his group begins to walk over to where Max and Tito are sitting.

1. What do Max and Tito infer from the nonverbal communication expressed by the other group of boys?

2. What message does Max's eye contact to Tito convey? What is Max trying to communicate to his friend by nodding to the other group of boys?

3. What is Tito trying to communicate to the other boys by staring at them with a menacing scowl?

4. What are some of the channels of nonverbal communication displayed in this encounter?

5. In your opinion, based on the information in the textbook, are these communicators responsibly managing their nonverbal communication? Why or why not?

SELF-TEST

For each of the following sentences, circle T if the statement is true or F if the statement is false.

T　F　1. Actions speak louder than words.

T　F　2. The more intimate you are with someone, the more nonverbal communication you share.

T　F　3. Kinesics is the study of eye contact and space.

T　F　4. Alexis and Makayla walk with their arms around each other. This is an example of love-intimacy touch.

T　F　5. Gwen tells Hale that she isn't interested in him, but she is always flirting with him. This is an example of a mixed message.

T   F   6. Shea writes down all her appointments and is never late. This is an example of P-time orientation.

T   F   7. According to the definition of personal space in the textbook, if someone is "invading your personal space," they are six inches or closer to you.

T   F   8. You can exude power through physical appearance.

T   F   9. Raising your hand in class is an example of a regulator.

T   F   10. Maricella wears Hector's letterman's jacket to show they are exclusively dating. This is an example of an affect display.

T   F   11. Alina owns expensive purses and shoes and drives a Mercedes-Benz. These are artifacts that may influence others to believe she is rich.

T   F   12. You can exert dominance over someone by using silence.

T   F   13. A fast-food restaurant's hard seats and harsh lighting are an example of how emblems can cause customers to eat quickly and leave right away.

T   F   14. Kyle, Chad, and Chase are at the movies. While Chad and Chase go to buy some popcorn, Kyle puts his coat over the other two seats to indicate that they're reserved. This is an example of territoriality.

T   F   15. Eli is giving Katie the silent treatment after getting into an argument the night before. Eli is using haptics to represent anger.

T   F   16. Jason has the habit of pulling his left ear while talking to people for the first time. This is an example of an adaptor.

T   F   17. June shakes her new coworker's hand. This is an example of functional-professional touch.

T   F   18. Increased eye contact, nodding, and smiling are all nonverbal ways to communicate immediacy.

T   F   19. The socially acceptable distance that we keep between ourselves and others during conversation varies from culture to culture.

T   F   20. Loudness, a characteristic of vocalics, can be adapted to online communication.

JOURNAL ENTRY

Which of the eight nonverbal communication codes are you most aware of using when meeting a potential friend for the first time? A potential romantic interest? Describe a recent interpersonal interaction when you reacted negatively to someone's nonverbal communication codes. Compare it to a time when you reacted positively to someone's nonverbal communication codes. What do these interactions tell you about your own cultural expectations for nonverbal communication?

STUDY OUTLINE

Fill in the blanks to complete the outline.

I. Conflict and Interpersonal Communication

    A. **Conflict** is a transactional process between people who perceive _____,

    _____, and _____.

        1. Conflict unfolds _____.

        2. Conflict is strongly shaped by _____.

        3. Conflicts are rooted in our perceptions regarding _____.

    B. Most conflicts occur between people who know each other and are involved in close

    relationships.

        1. The information you and your romantic partners share with each other bonds you

           together and it also provides _____ .

        2. When romantic partners engage in **kitchen-sinking**, they _____

           _____.

        3. The _____ investment we make in our close relationships further adds

           to the complexity of the conflict.

II. Power and Conflict

    A. **Power** is the ability to _____ other people and events.

        1. Power is _____ present.

           a. Relationships may be _____ in power (friend to friend) or

              _____ (manager to employee).

           b. Power-balanced relationships are called _____, while power-imbalanced

              relationships are called _____.

        2. Power can be used _____ or _____.

        3. Power is granted, meaning that individuals or groups allow another people or group to

           _____ over them.

        4. Power _____ most conflicts.

    B. In order to acquire power, you must possess or control some form of _____.

        1. _____ currency includes material things such as money, property,

           food, and the like.

        2. **Expertise currency** comprises _____

           _____.

        3. A person who is linked with a circle of friends, family, and acquaintances has

           _____.

        4. Examples of **personal currency** are _____

           _____.

        5. **Intimacy currency** is _____.

    C. Views of power _____ across cultures.

1. The degree to which people view the unequal distribution of power as acceptable is known as _____.

2. Within high **power-distance** cultures, people give privileged treatment and extreme respect to those in _____.

3. In low power-distance cultures, people in high-status positions strive to _____ _____.

D. Throughout history and across cultures, the defining distinction between the genders has been _____.

1. Through patriarchy, men have used cultural practices to maintain their _____, _____, and _____ power.

2. Women have lower _____, _____, and _____ power.

III. Approaching Conflict

A. When you ignore or communicate ambiguously about a situation where conflict can arise it is called _____.

1. One common form is **skirting**, which occurs when _____ _____.

2. Another is called _____, or communicating in a negative fashion and then _____.

3. _____ occurs when our repressed annoyances grow.

4. A **pseudo-conflict**, on the other hand, is _____ _____.

100

B. Through **accommodation**, one person abandons _____ _____.

C. _____ is where you confront others and pursue your own goals to the exclusion of theirs.

    1. The primary risk of this approach is **escalation**, which is _____ _____.

    2. Escalation causes people to use _____ or _____, both of which can permanently damage a relationship.

D. _____ is the most constructive form of conflict management.

    1. Communicators treat conflict as a _____ _____.

    2. To use a collaborative approach, openly discuss _____ or _____ that has fueled your conflict.

E. We often perceive our antagonists as _____ and ourselves as _____.

F. Both men and women use _____ as a strategy for dealing with conflict.

IV. Conflict Resolutions and Outcomes

A. Short-term conflict resolutions take one of four forms:

    1. The sudden withdrawal of one person from an encounter is called _____.

    2. **Domination** occurs when _____ _____.

3. Through _____ both parties change their goals to make them

compatible.

4. Both sides preserve and attain their goals by developing a creative solution to their

problem through _____.

B. Certain approaches for dealing with conflict strongly predict _____

_____.

    1. People who use _____ have lower relationship satisfaction and

endure longer and more frequent conflicts than people who _____.

    2. People who use _____ experience much better long-term

outcomes.

C. Part of effectively managing conflict is accepting that _____

_____.

V. Gender and Culture's Influence on Conflict

A. Our perceptions of a conflict and the move we make during a dispute are

_____.

    1. Women are encouraged to avoid and suppress conflict and to sacrifice _____

_____.

    2. Men learn to adopt _____ approaches

to interpersonal conflict.

    3. A **demand-withdraw pattern** occurs when _____

_____.

B. Belonging to a(n) _____ or _____

culture is the strongest cultural influence on how you approach conflict.

1. Collectivist cultures often view direct messages regarding conflict as

   _____.

2. People raised in individualistic cultures feel comfortable _____.

VI. The Challenge of Managing Conflict and Power

   A. Though conflicts carry risk, they also provide _____

   _____.

   B. The distinguishing feature between conflict and power struggles that destroy and those that

   create opportunities for improvement is _____

   _____.

WORD SEARCH

Each of the following clues is a key term from Chapter 9. Write the term in the space provided, and then find it hidden in the word search.

1. When Samara saw Aidan at the grocery store, she immediately ducked behind a display of pasta

   sauce because she never paid him back the $100 she borrowed from him a month ago. This way

   of handling conflict is called _____.

2. Aslan knows the bouncer at a very posh and elite nightclub. This kind of power is known as

   social _____ currency.

3. When Georgie and Kim were on the verge of breaking up, they instead went to counseling,

   completely changed the way they communicated, and redefined their roles in the relationship.

   These changes are called _____ improvements.

4. Celine confronts her coworker Dorian after work and angrily argues that he should not pursue a

   promotion that she thinks she deserves. Celine is engaging in _____ as a

   way of handling conflict while pursuing her own goals.

5. Jamie has been irritated with Lawrence for weeks. Lawrence never cleans up, always leaves dirty dishes in the kitchen, and doesn't put the groceries away. When he leaves the living room a mess one day, Jamie snipes at him and a fight ensues. Jamie's built-up irritation grew into _____ annoyance.

6. When Cole and Miranda can't decide what kind of car to buy—a mini-van or an SUV— Cole persuades Miranda that vans are safer, more practical, and more economical than her choice, an SUV, and she gives in because he makes more money than she does. Cole and Miranda's conflict was resolved through _____.

7. On a recent plane trip, Jacquie was the only doctor on board when a passenger began having a heart attack. In this situation, Jacquie had _____ currency.

8. Marlon and Josh are fighting about whose turn it is to play video games. Josh bolts out of the room and goes outside to play basketball. This sudden withdrawal which results in short-term conflict resolution is called _____.

```
J I B Z K I V V W N G O J Z U L K H A S Z C
H V X X P C Q C O A V O I D A N C E B W O G
Q H R L S P J I X A U Y W F O Z B W Y M W S
O D M F D O T K J E X V T E Y G I E P A A J
L H H P W A V I O W H X I K M Z G E K O S F
F G P A R N G Z A L D S Y T I C T C N J D U
A I B A N E X R V S U K S Z L I I P P W K H
U U P S O O X W K E P A I Q T I R X M A D F
S E M R I D P P N U V Y D I I Q M G C L D N
S X D T T W N Q E J W I O L M H A K N T G Z
P P N E A J B E T R J N T L X L H T D S W H
D D O J N P X C W S T V K A D D D C M D N H
G Z Q G I R A A O T Q I E N L L B R B A Z B
M F I N M V E P R J T G S Y T U I R R U U W
Q S Z S O C M P K J W L B E X P M N K R J G
J O M M D A U Q B K M D W L G M C U E F I R
L A R U T C U R T S G U L E O P A T C G O I
K V I M M U X R O D N F G L T J Q B Y A T K
Z Y I Y W X T Y E J N S H H L A Z F U Z N P
Y U O K Y Z T V V Y F O M Q N Y Q J U R C I
D M J Q G K G I G Y Z I A T M J K J W U U K
D Z I U I M S K S C S U H M Y L M P O Y K Z
```

DEFINING KEY TERMS

Write a sentence that defines each of the following key terms.

1. Conflict _____

_____

2. Kitchen-sinking

_____

3. Power _____

_____

4. Complementary relationships _____

_____

5. Resource currency _____

_____

6. Power-distance _____

_____

7. Skirting _____

_____

8. Pseudo-conflict _____

_____

9. Accommodation _____

_____

10. Escalation _____

_____

11. Collaboration _____

_____

12. Integrative agreements _____

_____

CASE STUDY

Read and analyze the following case study, and then answer the questions regarding conflict and power in communication.

Matt and Christine are married and run a chiropractic practice together. Christine is the chiropractor, and Matt manages the office. At home, Matt and Christine make an extra effort to be fair, equal, and balanced in all aspects of their life, from housework to decision-making. At work, they also try to make decisions together, but since Christine is the doctor, she often has the ultimate word in any disagreement.

One day at work, Matt gets into a heated argument with a client over the phone. The client claims that he should not have to pay a bill because he never received an invoice. The client is being irrational and uncooperative. Matt tells the client that he is no longer welcome at their practice and hangs up on him. Christine is furious at Matt for being so unprofessional. At home that night, Matt asks Christine if she is mad at him and she says she isn't, but she is especially short with him, eats dinner without him, and sleeps in the spare bedroom. Matt does not want to argue with Christine, so he doesn't say anything about the cold way she is treating him.

1. Power is present in Matt and Christine's relationship in all contexts. Are Matt and Christine's positions of power within the household different from their positions of power in the workplace? How and why?

2. What types of power currencies does Christine have over Matt in the workplace? Does she have the same power currencies at home?

3. What type of conflict style does Matt exhibit with the client? What types of conflict style does he exhibit with Christine?

4. What types of conflict style does Christine exhibit with Matt?

5. Give an example of how both Matt and Christine can use a collaborative approach for managing conflicts.

SELF-TEST

For each of the following sentences, circle T if the statement is true or F if the statement is false.

T   F   1. Marcia is so tired of arguing with her roommate over who has to clean the bathroom, she just gives in and decides to clean it herself. This is an example of avoidance.

T   F   2. The key to collaboration is giving equal attention to both people involved.

T   F   3. Competition involves confrontation.

T   F   4. An example of a complementary relationship is one between a boss and an employee.

T   F   5. Another term for a complementary relationship is a symmetrical relationship.

T　F　6. Sniping involves attacking a person and then eliminating the opportunity for him or her to respond.

T　F　7. When Sean yells, "Don't bother to ever call me again!" at his new girlfriend, this is an example of a sudden-death statement.

T　F　8. In a compromise, both parties must sacrifice their goals to some degree.

T　F　9. Conflict is a linear process.

T　F　10. Chloe tells Nadine that her feelings are hurt by something Nadine said the night before. Nadine immediately makes a joke about how sensitive Chloe is. This is an example of pseudo-conflict.

T　F　11. Nina's husband is a famous football player. This gives her social network currency.

T　F　12. At one time, Priscilla and Brent were both unhappy with the roles they played in their relationship. But then Brent decided to stay home to raise their sons while Priscilla took a high-paying job to support the family. Now they hardly ever fight about money or household chores. The changes Priscilla and Brent have made are called structural improvements.

T　F　13. Power-distance means that the more power you are perceived to have, the further away people tend to stand away from you while communicating.

T　F　14. Mea's mom takes away a toy every time Mea is naughty. The power that Mea's mom has is an example of resource currency.

T　F　15. Competition, as a way of handling conflict, is generally healthy for a relationship.

T　F　16. In close relationships, when a woman confronts a man in a conflict, the man usually retreats. This is called the demand-withdraw pattern.

T　F　17. Mike and Kate are arguing about Mike's staying out too late. Kate adds, "Not only do you stay out too late, you never help out with the kids. and you can't even wash your own dishes!" This is an example of kitchen-sinking.

T　F　18. Dirty secrets are false accusations aimed at intentionally causing conflict.

T　F　19. Joan and her friends are outside talking when Alex walks up to join the conversation. Just then, Joan walks away. Alex thinks Joan is angry with him, but in reality, Joan just doesn't like his cigarette smoke. This is an example of pseudo-conflict.

T　F　20. An integrative agreement is based on collaboration.

JOURNAL ENTRY

The text describes how gender and culture typically affect the way an individual approaches conflict. Reflect on your own conflict management style(s). To what extent do you think your gender and culture explain your personal style? In what ways? Cite some specific examples. What do you think are the greatest influences on how you've come to manage conflict in your life?

CHAPTER 10

Relationships with Romantic Partners

STUDY OUTLINE

Fill in the blanks to complete the outline.

I. Defining Romantic Relationships

    A. _____ is a feeling of affection and respect, whereas

        _____ is a deeper and more intense emotional commitment that

        consists of three components: _____, _____,

        and _____.

    B. **Passionate love** is a state of _____

        _____.

        1. Passionate love is driven by _____.

        2. No _____ differences exist in people's experience of

           passionate love.

        3. People from _____ feel passionate love.

        4. For adults, passionate love is integrally linked with _____ and

           _____.

        5. Passionate love is negatively related to _____

           _____.

6. **Companionate love** is _____

_____ .

7. The six **colors of love** are _____ , _____ ,

_____ , _____ ,

_____ , and _____ .

C. A **romantic relationship** is a _____

_____ ,

and it has four key elements.

1. A romantic relationship exists whenever the two partners _____

_____ .

2. In romantic relationships, we select whom we initiate involvements with but also

_____ and _____ we maintain these bonds.

3. Romantic relationships exhibit diversity in _____

_____ as well as _____

_____ .

4. Romantic relationships are forged through _____

_____ .

II. Romantic Attraction

A. **Social exchange theory** proposes that you'll feel drawn to those _____

_____ .

B. Proximity, or being in _____

exerts more impact on romantic attraction than many people think. This is known as the

_____ effect.

C. The **beautiful-is-good effect** suggests that we _____

_____.

    1. We tend to avoid forming long-term relationships with those we find _____

    _____, a phenomenon known as

    _____.

D. Evidence suggests that we are attracted to those we perceive as _____

_____, a phenomenon known as the

_____.

III. Relationship Development and Deterioration

A. Mark Knapp suggests that there are ten relational stages, which start with the five coming

    together stages.

    1. During the **initiating** stage, you _____

    _____.

    2. In the **experimenting** stage, _____

    _____.

    3. In the **intensifying** stage, the depth of _____ increases.

    4. During the **integrating** stage, you and your partner's personalities _____

    _____.

    5. **Bonding** is a _____ that announces your commitment.

B. The second half of Knapp's theory consists of the five coming apart stages.

    1. **Differentiating** is when the beliefs, attitudes, and values that distinguish you from your

    partner come to _____.

    2. **Circumscribing** is characterized by _____

    _____.

3. **Stagnating** is where both people presume that _____

_____.

4. In the **avoiding** stage, one or both of you decide _____

_____.

5. During the **terminating** stage, _____

_____.

IV. Maintaining Romantic Relationships

   A. **Relational maintenance** refers to _____

_____.

     1. Positivity includes _____

_____.

     2. Through openness, you create _____

_____.

     3. Assurances are messages that emphasize _____

_____.

     4. Happy committed couples develop _____ and make an effort to

_____.

     5. Sharing tasks involves jointly _____

_____.

     6. Social networks play a role in the survival in a relationship because _____

_____.

   B. Strategies for confronting relationship crises differ along two dimensions: the degree to

which they are _____ and the degree to which they are

_____.

1. The **voice strategy** is an active, constructive approach where _____ _____.

2. The **loyalty strategy** involves avoiding _____ _____, and if your partner raises a concern, you _____ _____.

3. The **exit strategy** is an _____ approach that involves _____ _____.

4. The **neglect strategy** is a passive, destructive approach where you _____ _____.

C. Four factors appear to be most important in predicting survival of romantic relationships:

1. _____ _____.

2. _____ _____.

3. _____ _____.

4. _____ _____.

V. The Dark Side of Romantic Relationships

A. **Dysfunctional relationship beliefs** are harmful _____ about _____.

1. One dysfunctional relationship belief is that all disagreement is _____.

2. Also, many believe that mind-reading is _____.

3. Third is the notion that _____

_____.

4. Fourth, people often believe that that every sexual encounter with a romantic partner

should be _____.

5. Finally, people believe that men and women are _____

_____ in their perceptions, emotions, and communication.

B. **Jealousy** is a protective reaction to a _____

_____.

   1. One jealousy-reducing strategy is called _____, which means

allowing yourself to feel jealous but not letting whatever sparked your jealousy interrupt

what you already were doing.

   2. Another commonly used strategy is self-bolstering, which is _____

_____.

   3. The last jealousy-reducing strategy is called selective ignoring, which means _____

_____.

C. **Betrayal** is an intentional action that _____

_____.

   1. The damage from betrayal comes mostly from _____, or the

realization that our partner _____.

   2. _____ is the most destructive form of romantic betrayal.

   3. _____ is intentional misrepresentation and is almost as damaging

to a relationship as infidelity.

WORD SEARCH

Each of the following clues is a key term from Chapter 10. Write the term in the space provided, and then find it hidden in the word search.

1. Suki and Kevin have a wedding ceremony. This is the _____ stage of a relationship.

2. Keith starts working later and later hours so that he won't have to go home and be with his wife. This is an example of the _____ stage of a relationship.

3. Jason and Peter believe that all aspects of their relationship should be fair and balanced. This is an example of _____.

4. Roshanna knows that what she feels for Melvin is deeper than liking him. She feels an intense emotional commitment of intimacy, caring, and attachment known as _____.

5. Sydney and Wyatt are in a stressful point in their relationship with money problems and a newborn baby, but they believe that once the baby gets older, things will get easier. This is known as the _____ strategy.

6. Craig starts to feel more and more attracted to Rhonda as they spend more and more time together in yoga class. Craig's growing attraction can be explained by the mere _____ effect.

7. Cerina thinks that she and Vincent were made for each other; they can hardly keep their hands off one another and feel lonely when they're apart even for a few hours. This is an example of _____ love.

8. Karen is distraught to find out that Julie has been spending their retirement money on frivolous things and lying to her about it. The pain and disappointment she feels because Julie doesn't respect her as much as she expected is called _____ devaluation.

```
W P C D I D W Y X K B P K O S R E N J O J R
S O V A L N W S G P D O A C E M M P F V M E
Y M Q O L V D O A T Q I H S J U H L F P Z L
Z V J G Y E W D Q Z R G W K S Y H Y H R Y A
T R L I B V Y D X V W A S G T I F J R T T T
N W B K K E T Z Y W V I G I B G O N S V Q I
E R U S O P X E J M B N U D E N R N V O C O
L O V I N G R B K D B Q Q Y H V Z Y A B D N
J D P L Z I K A G G E L Y X I J V O X T I A
E D P O A E V P N U A Q D F I Y R L J W E L
A J S S X P U J Q M A G P U D E Y I A E X P
S U G H R W L T O T P J N R U O L R K G F M
C B A M Z Y Y B G I G D N I S R C F Y G T E
H B D R C E N X P N L N W K D O U G T Z E H
B X T T D K C G K R A J N P E N Q R L N O O
C C P H M G N V J V M L H Q E F O R A M S K
W Q E P W N F T O C D X E E U K N B Y Z I G
V R M I I H M I X A J C Y T X M T M O Q Y S
T J G M O U D F G I H D X M X L S C L F J W
G I L L D I E W B P V G K J J F U S C X H S
Y H Q M N L P P A S F T A X N I W S I P G D
H D T G T R Q N U L U U Y M P Y A B T G D R
```

DEFINING KEY TERMS

Write a sentence that defines each of the following key terms.

1. Companionate love _____

_____

2. Romantic relationship _____

_____

3. Social exchange theory _____

_____

4. Initiating _____

_____

5. Beautiful-is-good effect _____

_____

6. Birds-of-a-feather effect _____

_____

7. Integrating _____

_____

8. Circumscribing _____

_____

9. Relational maintenance _____

_____

10. Voice strategy _____

_____

11. Neglect strategy _____

_____

12. Dysfunctional relationship beliefs _____

_____

CASE STUDY

Read and analyze the following case study, and then answer the questions regarding communication in romantic relationships.

Kristy and Amir and have been dating for four years and have fallen into a comfortable but predictable routine. Although their relationship no longer has the "spark" that it once did, Kristy feels a quiet sense of contentment. Amir, however, has been feeling that they are in a rut, that there is no more excitement in their relationship, and that things have become mundane. Because of his negative feelings about their relationship, he has been spending less and less time with Kristy and spending more time with his friends.

Then, Kristy gets a new roommate, Sheila. When Amir meets Sheila, he feels that she is pretty in a plain kind of way, and he isn't particularly attracted to her. As Amir sees Sheila more and more when he visits Kristy, he begins to feel drawn to her. Amir begins to e-mail Sheila, and they talk on the phone when Kristy is at work. One day, Kristy happens to see an e-mail from Amir to Sheila stating all of his negative feelings about his relationship with Kristy. Kristy feels betrayed and angry and accuses Amir of being unfaithful. Amir says that Kristy is just jealous and that she has no right to be angry because nothing has happened between him and Sheila.

1. What stages of relational development are Kristy and Amir going through in this scenario?

2. Why do you think Amir begins to feel more and more attracted to Sheila, even though at the beginning he doesn't feel that she is exceptionally good-looking?

3. Has Amir cheated on Kristy? Support your answer.

4. Why does Kristy feel so betrayed by Amir? How does emotional devaluation play a role in her feelings?

5. What types of strategies could Kristy and Amir use to approach this problem collaboratively?

SELF-TEST

For each of the following sentences, circle T if the statement is true or F if the statement is false.

T   F   1. Betrayal can be unintentional.

T   F   2. The beautiful-is-good effect states that the more attractive we perceive our romantic partner to be, the harder we try to resolve relationship problems.

T   F   3. Vinny arrives home to find that Margaret has moved out, taking all of her belongings. This is the terminating stage of their relationship.

T   F   4. The voice strategy involves voicing one's opinion in a forceful way; therefore, it is a destructive strategy.

T   F   5. Small talk involves light conversation about "safe" topics.

T   F   6. Relational maintenance is necessary for a relationship to endure.

T   F   7. You can become attracted to someone merely by being around him or her a lot.

T   F   8. Relational devaluation occurs when people in troubled relationships make negative comments toward one another.

T   F   9. Passionate love almost always evolves into companionate love over time.

T   F   10. Myla believes that, in time, her parents will come to accept her romantic relationship with Mayette. This is an example of a passive approach.

T   F   11. Jealousy is a reaction to a romantic partner's inappropriate behavior.

T   F   12. If you have low self-esteem and feel that you are not very good-looking, according to the matching phenomenon you will have the tendency to be attracted to a person that you perceive to be not very good-looking as well.

T   F   13. Phillip adores Jean and thinks she is his soul mate. Jean, however, has no clue he feels this way and considers Phillip a friend. Theirs can still be considered a romantic relationship.

T   F   14. According to the text, people seek out romantic partners who make up for the traits they lack.

T   F   15. Social exchange theory states that we are attracted to those who we feel have a lot to offer us with relatively few costs.

T   F   16. The colors of love describe the varying intensities people can feel in attraction, from liking to obsession.

T   F   17. Being positive in your communication with your romantic partner is an effective relational maintenance tactic.

T   F   18. Whether or not your friends approve of your romantic partner has no effect on your relationship.

T   F   19. Men and women are fundamentally different in the way they perceive and deal with romantic relationships.

T   F   20. If you experience unsatisfying sexual experiences with your romantic partner, your relationship is doomed.

JOURNAL ENTRY

Describe a relationship problem where you have used an active strategy. Was it a destructive or constructive approach? Were you successful at resolving the problem? Now, describe a relationship problem where you utilized a passive strategy. Was it a destructive or constructive approach? Compare and contrast the strategies, and describe the outcomes of each situation. What would you do differently, if anything, in each situation?

_____

_____

_____

_____

_____

_____

_____

_____

_____

_____

_____

_____

_____

_____

_____

_____

CHAPTER 11
Relationships with Family and Friends

STUDY OUTLINE

Fill in the blanks to complete the outline.

I. Defining Family

   A. **A family** is a group of people who _____

     _____.

   B. There are five characteristics that distinguish families from other social groups:

     1. Families create a sense of _____ through interpersonal

       communication.

     2. Because we forge family relationships during an early and very impressionable period

       in our lives, these bonds often prove _____.

     3. Families use interpersonal communication to _____ both

       inside the family and in ways that can distinguish _____

       _____.

     4. Families share a _____.

     5. Family members often share _____ material, which can lead to

       shared _____ as well as similar _____,

       _____, and _____.

C. There is no such thing as the _____ American family.

    1. The _____ family, which represents a minority in the United

       States, consists of a wife, husband, and their biological or adopted children.

    2. A **gay** or **lesbian family** consists of _____

       _____.

    3. An **extended family** results when relatives such as _____

       _____ live together in a common household.

    4. **Blended families** result from _____ and include _____

       _____.

    5. _____ consist of two unmarried, romantically involved adults

       living together in a household, with or without children.

    6. In a _____ family, only one adult possesses sole responsibility for

       one or more children.

D. **Family communication patterns** are beliefs about _____

    _____ and the resulting interpersonal communication from

these beliefs.

    1. **Conversation orientation** is _____

       _____.

      a. Families with high conversation orientation establish and practice family rituals,

        which are _____

        _____.

      b. Families with a low conversation orientation view interpersonal communication as

        _____.

2. **Conformity orientation** is the degree to which families use communication to _____

_____.

    a. Families with high conformity use their interactions to highlight and enforce

      _____.

    b. Families with low conformity communicate in ways that emphasize _____

      _____.

3. The four family communication patterns are _____,

_____, _____, and

_____.

II. Maintaining Family Relationships

    A. In order for family relationships to be sustained, they _____

_____.

    B. Three strategies for maintaining romances can also be applied to family maintenance.

They are _____, _____, and _____.

    C. The two dialectics especially pronounced in families are _____

and _____.

      1. The struggle between autonomy and connection is especially pronounced during

_____.

      2. If parents and children have forged close relationships before teens begin to assert their

autonomy, young people are likely to view their family as their _____

_____.

      3. The balance between openness versus protection is typically defined through

_____, which are _____

_____.

D. Family stories are _____

_____.

    1. Some examples of types of family stories are _____,

      _____, and _____ stories.

    2. When telling family stories, one should typically avoid stories that breach

      _____ and that make fun of family members in ways

      _____.

E. When managing family conflict, the lessons that we learn will be mirrored in _____

_____.

    1. **Avoidant families** pretend that _____

      _____.

    2. In **aggressive families**, parents teach children to _____

      _____.

    3. **Collaborative families** deal with conflict _____ and encourage

      _____

      _____.

III. Defining Friendship

A. All **friendships** are voluntary interpersonal relationships in which _____

_____.

    1. You have the privilege of _____ your friends, and this is how

      friendships differ from family.

    2. People from different cultures have _____

      _____ regarding friendships.

B. Friendships take different forms, yet they all help us fulfill two primary interpersonal

  needs: _____ and _____.

  1. **Communal friendships** focus primarily on _____

     _____.

  2. **Agentic friendships** focus primarily on _____

     _____.

C. Contrary to the common stereotype, male and female same-gender friendships are more

  _____ than they are _____.

  1. Euro-American men, unlike women, learn to avoid _____

     _____.

  2. A radical shift in relationship patterns over the last few decades has been the increase of

     _____ relationships.

     a. Most cross-gender friendships are not motivated by _____.

     b. Two challenges men and women face in forming cross-gender relationships are that

        _____ and

        _____

        _____.

D. In **friends-with-benefits (FWB) relationships**, participants _____

  _____.

  1. One reason that men and women form FWB relationships is _____

     _____.

  2. The second reason men and women form FWB relationships is to _____

     _____.

3. Despite clear rules regarding emotional attachment, communication and sex, most FWB

relationships eventually _____.

IV. Maintaining Friendship Relationships

A. One strategy to maintain friendships is to share activities, in other words, _____

_____.

1. Another strategy in friendship maintenance is openness, as all friendships are created

and maintained through _____

_____.

B. Another strategy for friendship maintenance is abiding by **friendship rules,** which are

_____

_____.

C. Some of the friendship rules as stated in the textbook are: _____,

_____, _____, and

_____.

D. Physical separation prevents both communal and agentic friends from adequately

_____

_____; therefore, geographic separation is the

most frequently cited reason for deterioration of friendships.

1. In friendships that survive geographic separation, the two people feel particularly strong

_____ for each other.

2. Friends who survive separation also accept _____ as a natural part

of life and their relationship.

3. Last, friends who survive separation have a strong sense of _____.

128

V. The Primacy of Family and Friends

  A. Relationships with both family and friends survive only if you invest _____

    _____.

  B. We often neglect to communicate with our family and friends because _____

    _____ compared to romantic relationships.

  C. Friends and family can help us charge forward, even though we're afraid or discouraged.

WORD SEARCH

Each of the following clues is a key term from Chapter 11. Write the term in the space provided, and then find it hidden in the word search.

1. Andre and Kelly are romantic partners and live together, but they are not married. They are an

    example of a(n) _____ couple.

2. The Price family is trying to decide where to go for their annual family vacation. They believe

    that they should all agree on the destination. With their high level of conformity and

    conversation orientation, the Price family is considered a(n) _____

    family.

3. Shelly lives in a home with her mother, father, brother, and grandmother. Their household is

    considered a(n) _____ family.

4. Roger and Liza have agreed that they will remain strictly friends, but once in awhile they engage

    in sexual activity. This is an example of a(n) _____ relationship.

5. Kitty's parents never include her in big decisions, and their family never has family talks. Her

    parents expect her to not deviate too much from the standards they've set for her, and she doesn't

    have much desire to express herself in family matters. Kitty's family is an example of a(n)

    _____ family.

6. Regina and Rose are friends who go out to lunch together once a week, play tennis on the weekends, and talk on the telephone every night. This is an example of a(n) _____ friendship.

7. When Lee and Bren formed a study group for school, they formed a(n) _____ friendship.

8. Rhea often tells the story of how her two oldest sons used to sit on their younger brother and tickle him until he told them where he hid his candy. This is an example of a family _____.

```
C S Y B X R F E F A P D G K L C Y V V A B K
L O E S E J V L D C P A B V R U I Q X P Y T
G S N F F H M R W J R G K P Q F I T S B D I
L O S S V Y R W B E O G Q K I M B E N K E F
F C G Y E J R M K O T O Q A W R O R U E L W
G B V M H N K O Y X E V X M Z V H Y M T G E
L N J T W Z S V R F C U J T F L S R A T D A
X S E R E K W U R G T L A N U M M O C I C D
Q D C F M Q J D A O I C I R G M Y T K E G C
T X C S T V E J J L V I M D G K M S S D F Z
R C C J B U R E U H E W B O B B W S J Y C S
M R B S C D X U B N N W U Y P L X H T R R C
K W U S S T T Z S H F L W T O V H T X T W M
O R T B E G I P D O G V X D J G P L J Q I Q
X Z W N R C N X T O L O W G N A T A E M C Y
V M D T K F C P A K Y F Y O Y E O K N J H P
F E R N Q E V D S G P Z E G B S U C K X T Z
D T G O W G L J A O O I I I O P Y I I G J J
L K P V W Y O D G V C C P H V Z W B A R V B
N A T Y H T S R N A Z U P T J F X L Y Z I D
A M X U J S C O H A B I T A T I N G J S Q F
P I Z O Q I E V K Q T V M G U I V Q F K S A
```

DEFINING KEY TERMS

Write a sentence that defines each of the following key terms.

1. **Nuclear family** _____

_____

2. Blended family _____

_____

3. Family communication patterns _____

_____

4. Conversation orientation _____

_____

5. Conformity orientation _____

_____

6. Pluralistic families _____

_____

7. Laissez-faire families _____

_____

8. Family communication rules _____

_____

9. Avoidant families _____

_____

10. Aggressive families _____

_____

11. Collaborative families _____

_____

12. Friendship rules _____

_____

CASE STUDY

Read and analyze the following case study, and then answer the questions regarding communication in family relationships.

Victoria grew up in a family where children were meant to be seen and not heard. Her parents rarely involved her and her brother in important decisions, and they never had family talks. Her parents discouraged the voicing of opinions because they enforced the idea that the family should all live by traditional values. Because of the absence of communication between Victoria and her parents, Victoria's parents were never aware of her struggle with her identity and just assumed that Victoria's best friend, Deb, was solely that—a friend. But when she was a senior in high school, Victoria shared with her family that she was gay. Victoria also told her parents that her plan was to move out of their house after graduation and move in with Deb and Deb's one-year-old daughter.

1. Growing up, what was Victoria's family's conversation orientation? What do you think was Victoria's major concern with telling her parents about her sexual orientation?

2. What factors might have made it difficult for Victoria's family to realize that she was gay?

3. Compare and contrast the type of family environment in which Victoria grew up with the type of family she likely will have when she moves in with Deb and her daughter.

4. Given their family communication style, how do you think Victoria's family will react to this news?

5. What communication strategies can Victoria's family use to maintain family relationships?

SELF-TEST

For each of the following sentences, circle T if the statement is true or F if the statement is false.

T   F   1. The majority of families in the United States consist of a mother, a father, and a child (or children).

T   F   2. Any couple is considered a family.

T   F   3. Friendships can happen involuntarily.

T   F   4. Laissez-faire families are characterized by low levels of conformity and conversation orientation.

T   F   5. The two components of family communication patterns are how much or little conversation and conformity are expected in the family.

T   F   6. Val, Donn, and Willie often retell the story about how they set fire to their dad's favorite green chair. This is an example of a family story.

T   F   7. Shea and Jade enjoy going shopping, drinking coffee, and going on long walks with each other. This is an example of an agentic friendship.

T   F   8. A cohabiting couple is another term for a blended family.

T F 9. Conformity orientation deals with the degree to which family members believe that emotion-sharing is important.

T F 10. The Rios household consists of the mother, the father, two sons, and the grandmother. This is an example of an extended family.

T F 11. There are four different family communication patterns: consensual, pluralistic, protective, and laissez-faire.

T F 12. The collaborative approach to resolving family conflicts is better than the avoidant and aggressive approaches.

T F 13. Friends-with-benefits relationships normally work out well if there are clear rules about the friendship from the beginning.

T F 14. Typically, communication technologies may help maintain friendships that face geographic separation.

T F 15. One of the differences between family relationships and friendships is that friendships are voluntary.

T F 16. Sean and Norman work out together on a regular basis, helping "spot" each other while lifting weights, motivating each other, and giving each other fitness tips. They never hang out outside the gym. Theirs is an agentic relationship.

T F 17. Annie and Howard never discuss finances, their careers, or big decisions with their children. They are a family low in conversation orientation.

T F 18. Collaborative families handle conflict indirectly, which is a less effective strategy for dealing with conflict.

T F 19. Marissa talks to her brother Mark about their childhood dog, Oreo, all the time, but she never talks to her sister Maryann about Oreo because Maryann tends to get very emotional about the topic. This is an example of a family communication pattern.

T F 20. By the sixth grade, same-sex friends have become our primary source of emotional support over our families.

134

JOURNAL ENTRY

Watch an episode of a TV show that involves a family, such as The Simpsons, The Family Guy, Everybody Hates Chris, *or* Gilmore Girls. *What is the structure of the family? What is their typical family communication pattern? What examples do they exhibit of their conversation and conformity orientation? What family communication rules do they exhibit? How is the family's communication part of the show?*

CHAPTER 12

Relationships in the
Workplace

Name: _____

Class: _____

Date: _____

STUDY OUTLINE

Fill in the blanks to complete the outline.

I. Defining Workplace Relationships

    A. A **workplace relationship** is _____

    _____.

    B. **Organizational culture** is a distinctive set of _____ .

       1. An organization's culture derives from the norms governing _____

       _____.

       2. Workplace artifacts, which also contribute to an organization's culture, are _____

       _____.

       3. Workplace values are _____

       _____.

    C. _____, or systems of communication linkages, are defined

    by three characteristics.

       1. The first characteristic is the _____

       _____ that flows through the network.

2. The second characteristic is the _____ through which the

information flows.

3. The frequency and number of connections among people in a network is known as

_____.

II. Supportive and Defensive Organizational Climates

A. A workplace's **organizational climate** is its _____ and is a product

of _____, _____, and

_____.

B. In **defensive climates**, workers describe the workplace environment as _____

_____.

C. **Supportive climates** are described as _____

_____.

D. Six characteristics of how people communicate determine an organization's climate.

1. _____ is the degree to which

communication seems well rehearsed or authentic.

2. _____ is the tendency to believe in only one solution, while

_____ is the willingness to question opinions and decisions in

conditional terms.

3. _____ is the degree to which

people communicate only to achieve their own goals versus taking others' perspectives

into account.

4. Evaluation versus description is _____

_____.

5. Detachment versus empathy is _____

_____.

6. In defensive climates, the power difference between employees is _____

_____, while supportive

climates try to _____.

E. Some strategies for creating a supportive climate are:

1. Encourage _____. to

2. Adopt _____.

3. _____ rather than _____.

4. Describe _____ rather than _____.

5. Offer _____ rather than _____.

6. Emphasize _____.

III. Peer Relationships

A. **Professional peers** are _____

_____.

1. Information peers are _____

_____.

2. Collegial peers are _____ relationships because _____

_____.

3. Special peers are _____

_____.

4. **Virtual peers** are _____

_____.

138

B. _____ and _____ are important tactics in

maintaining peer relationships.

1. Collegial and special peer relationships also grow stronger when _____

_____ and do not _____

_____.

C. One obstacle of cross-sex peers is that they must go to great lengths to _____

_____.

D. Workplace romances are formed generally between _____, and most

people feel that these relationships _____

_____.

IV. Mixed-Status Relationships

A. **Mixed-status relationships** are defined as _____

_____.

B. **Upward communication** is communication from _____

_____.

C. The most effective upward communication is _____, which is based

on six principles:

1. Plan before you _____.

2. Know why your supervisor should _____.

3. Tailor your _____.

4. Know your supervisor's _____.

5. Create coalitions _____.

6. Competently _____.

D. **Downward communication** is _____

_____.

E. Effective downward communication involves five principles:

   1. Routinely and openly emphasize the _____

   _____.

   2. _____ empathetically.

   3. Frame wants and needs as _____.

   4. Be sensitive to _____.

   5. Share _____ whenever possible.

F. How to effectively _____ and how to

   _____ are two challenges of downward communication.

   1. Compliments are most effective when they focus on _____

   _____.

   2. To offer constructive criticism:

     a. Open with _____ and end with _____.

     b. Follow the guidelines for _____

     and recommendations for _____.

G. Maintaining mixed status relationships requires you to _____

_____

_____ and to communicate in _____

_____.

H. **Workplace abuse** involves _____

_____.

1. Some scholars argue that workplace abuse causes more damage in an organization than

   sexual harassment because _____

   _____.

2. Some people deal with workplace abuse by _____, others

   _____, and some people _____

   _____.

I. **Sexual harassment** occurs in two forms in the workplace.

   1. Quid pro quo harassment is _____

      _____.

   2. Hostile climate harassment is _____

      _____.

   3. Some ways of coping with sexual harassment are _____

      _____, _____

      _____, or _____

      _____.

WORD SEARCH

Each of the following clues is a key term from Chapter 12. Write the term in the space provided, and then find it hidden in the word search.

1. Russell tries to persuade his office manager, Peter, to implement a new training schedule for the

   new employees. This is an example of _____.

2. Leon and Monica are coworkers who communicate via instant messaging all day. They are

   _____ peers.

3. Amanda, Glen, Mario, and Osmond are considered the young, hip, carefree group at their workplace. Their group is an example of a workplace _____.

4. Karen asks her boss for two weeks off. This is an example of _____ communication.

5. Jin and Trang both hold the title of Education Specialist II at their workplace. They are considered professional _____.

6. Aries, the restaurant manager, asks Jamie, a food server, to pick up his dry cleaning. When Jamie reluctantly agrees, Aries thanks her and slaps her on the behind. This is an example of _____ harassment.

7. Karina takes credit for the annual charity dinner that Emery planned and organized. This is an example of a workplace _____.

8. At VBS Business Solutions, employees feel discouraged and unsupported, and employee morale is low. This is a(n) _____ climate.

```
E F A E W J V I R T U A L D K M P Q R S J C
V C K M K R H D U Q G W S U F F I P P A P J
I N O H X G Q I C Z Q E U M T W V L Y I M S
S X K R E O R R W H X D R H I M K U A Z L M
N R A M E L N W Q U M F K E N J O J L M P Z
E J S K L R Z C A D R W D J E F U F J Q Q W
F H N G D Z Z L P H J O Z Y D L Z I A V A Z
E D O O G V C K P M O H P U B S P F Z N R R
D N U N P O N T T X H I K X S D K Z Y J Q N
B J I P P B M V O U Q U N L L H O C G P I E
S R E E P D Q I F K Y E P T V A A T K Y Z D
N X H Y C E N F T H H X Y C Z C Q M O X J D
C E M P G T T U J G I V D G O L D O F B D J
W L S K K T E P G C N S F V K X Q R T Z K O
P G I U J P B W M A T M D U X B F X N H B V
V N H Q B P L A H N K A O L Q X C A Q V S N
L S L J U A E R D M L H X G I R L G N W U Q
E P S W V E B D I C D F T P S L N D O S O S
B X A K D L N U N Z W D P Q P H D D D R K Q
A E R I B W S Q F J R W L C H Q N D P R R D
Q T F I T P Q R F B S D C X Y L H G J Y U W
I T K H X C K G E A U S Y G O R X G C L O V
```

DEFINING KEY TERMS

Write a sentence that defines each of the following key terms.

1. Workplace relationships _____

_____

2. Organizational culture _____

_____

3. Organizational networks _____

_____

4. Virtual networks _____

_____

5. Organizational climate _____

_____

6. Supportive climate _____

_____

7. Mixed-status relationships _____

_____

8. Downward communication _____

_____

9. Advocacy _____

_____

10. Workplace abuse _____

_____

11. Sexual harassment _____

_____

12. Virtual peers _____

_____

CASE STUDY

Read and analyze the following case study, and then answer the questions regarding communication in workplace relationships.

Trey is a lead engineer at a biotechnology firm. He supervises a group of four engineers and reports to Irene, the director of engineering. Trey and Irene have gotten along very well since Trey started working for the firm. Trey is an ambitious go-getter with a professional, positive attitude, as is Irene. Trey, Irene, and a few other upper- and middle-management employees often hang out outside of work. Due to recent budget concerns, the firm has begun to lay off some employees. Irene has empathetically and politely requested that Trey lay off two of the engineers who work under him. Trey does as he is asked. Weeks later, Trey's two remaining subordinates begin to complain to Trey about the workload. They claim that they have absorbed the work of the two laid-off employees and blame the upper management, including Irene. Trey's two remaining subordinates have been heard talking maliciously about the upper management in the break room and in the parking lot. Trey is conflicted because even though he doesn't agree with the manner in which his employees are handling the matter, he knows that they are, indeed, under a great amount of stress given the increased workload. Trey is unsure about what, if anything, to tell Irene.

1. What type of peer relationship exists between Trey and Irene? How does this affect their communication about work matters?

2. Describe how the formation and existence of workplace cliques plays a role in this scenario.

3. What strategies can Trey utilize in this scenario to effectively maintain his relationship with Irene?

4. How might the behavior of Trey's two remaining employees affect the workplace culture?

5. How could Trey's two remaining employees communicate their concerns in a more constructive way?

SELF-TEST

For each of the following sentences, circle T if the statement is true or F if the statement is false.

T F 1. Workplace cliques contribute to a decrease in worker productivity.

T F 2. Workplace cliques are defined as coworkers who interact regularly together outside the workplace.

T F 3. Organizational climates can either be defensive or supportive.

T F 4. Downward communication is defined as talking down to employees or being condescending.

T F 5. Sherwin and Ephraim are a couple who work at the same company. This is an example of a mixed-status relationship.

T F 6. Advocacy means standing up for what you think is right.

T F 7. Advanced Biometrics is a company that values working hard and playing hard. This mentality is part of their organizational culture.

T F 8. Doug, Lou, Lynn, and Mari are all on the "counselor list" on the company e-mail system, and they communicate regularly but only through e-mail. Theirs is a virtual network.

T F 9. Workplace relationships differ along three dimensions: status, intimacy, and equity.

T F 10. Quyen feels that she deserves a raise but is afraid to ask her boss because she feels he is unfriendly and inflexible, just like the company as a whole. This is an example of a defensive climate.

T F 11. Suzie and Miguel have daily debriefings to update each other on the status of their projects. This is an organizational network.

T F 12. Balance Credit Systems has an annual family picnic and gives all employees the day off, paid. This is a way for the company to help build a supportive climate.

T F 13. Upward communication travels from subordinate to superior.

T F 14. Cynthia repeatedly sends Carrie e-mails belittling her work at the office. This is an example of workplace abuse.

T F 15. Workplace abuse often stems from the power difference in mixed-status relationships.

T F 16. Workplace artifacts are physical objects that contribute to a organization's culture.

T F 17. The negative outcomes associated with workplace romances may be more pronounced for men than women.

T F 18. Effective downward communication is characterized by the willingness of people in power to communicate positively without relying on their power.

T F 19. Supervisors should not phrase wants and needs as requests because doing so relinquishes power.

T F 20. Floyd's boss often demands that he finish reports that normally take two to three hours in 20 minutes. This unreasonable request is a form of workplace abuse.

JOURNAL ENTRY

What do you think are the most important factors in building a positive working environment? Do you think that employee interaction outside the workplace helps or hinders productivity? Support your ideas, and cite specific examples.

ANSWER KEY

CHAPTER 1

1.	T	(p. 7)	8.	T	(p. 16)	15.	F	(p. 26)
2.	F	(p. 8)	9.	F	(p. 16)	16.	T	(p. 27)
3.	F	(p. 8)	10.	T	(pp. 17–18)	17.	F	(p. 31)
4.	T	(p. 10)	11.	T	(p. 20)	18.	F	(p. 31)
5.	F	(p. 10)	12.	F	(p. 21)	19.	F	(p. 25)
6.	T	(p. 12)	13.	T	(p. 21)	20.	F	(p. 32)
7.	F	(p. 13)	14.	T	(p. 23)			

CHAPTER 2

1.	F	(p. 58)	8.	T	(p. 52)	15.	F	(p. 71)
2.	F	(p. 59)	9.	T	(p. 64)	16.	T	(p. 59)
3.	T	(pp. 67–68)	10.	F	(pp. 61–62)	17.	T	(p. 66)
4.	T	(p. 59)	11.	T	(p. 71)	18.	F	(pp. 67–68)
5.	F	(pp. 44–47)	12.	T	(p. 74)	19.	F	(p. 68)
6.	T	(p. 55)	13.	T	(p. 70)	20.	F	(p. 49)
7.	T	(pp. 67–68)	14.	F	(p. 74)			

CHAPTER 3

1.	F	(p. 101)	8.	T	(p. 83)	15.	T	(p. 92)
2.	T	(p. 86)	9.	T	(p. 107)	16.	F	(p. 92)
3.	F	(p. 106)	10.	F	(p. 87)	17.	F	(p. 93)
4.	T	(p. 90)	11.	T	(p. 102)	18.	T	(pp. 96–98)
5.	F	(pp. 83–84)	12.	T	(p. 88)	19.	T	(p. 103)
6.	T	(p. 100)	13.	F	(p. 95)	20.	F	(p. 107)
7.	T	(p. 83)	14.	F	(p. 99)			

CHAPTER 4

1.	F	(pp. 122–123)	8.	F	(p. 132)	15.	T	(p. 133)
2.	F	(pp. 121–122)	9.	T	(p. 140)	16.	F	(p. 133)
3.	T	(p. 127)	10.	F	(p. 132)	17.	T	(pp. 141–142)
4.	F	(p. 140)	11.	T	(p. 131)	18.	T	(p. 142)
5.	T	(pp. 121–122)	12.	T	(p. 139)	19.	T	(pp. 122–123)
6.	T	(p. 141)	13.	T	(p. 121)	20.	T	(p. 123)
7.	T	(pp. 132–133)	14.	T	(p. 131)			

CHAPTER 5

1.	T	(p. 177)	8.	F	(p. 158)	15.	F	(p. 154)
2.	F	(p. 166)	9.	F	(p. 154)	16.	F	(p. 162)
3.	F	(p. 162)	10.	T	(p. 167)	17.	T	(p. 169)
4.	F	(p. 154)	11.	T	(p. 174)	18.	T	(p. 167)
5.	T	(p. 169)	12.	F	(p. 180)	19.	T	(p. 177)
6.	F	(p. 156)	13.	F	(p. 167)	20.	T	(p. 173)
7.	T	(p. 175)	14.	T	(p. 169)			

CHAPTER 6

1.	T	(p. 202)	8.	T	(p. 193)	15.	T	(p. 203)
2.	T	(p. 209)	9.	F	(p. 188)	16.	F	(p. 209)
3.	F	(p. 188)	10.	F	(p. 200)	17.	T	(p. 192)
4.	T	(p. 193)	11.	T	(p. 193)	18.	T	(p. 202)
5.	F	(p. 197)	12.	F	(p. 192)	19.	F	(p. 196)
6.	F	(p. 203)	13.	T	(p. 197)	20.	T	(p. 188)
7.	F	(p. 208)	14.	T	(p. 212)			

CHAPTER 7

1.	T	(p. 222)	8.	T	(p. 225)	15.	T	(p. 121)
2.	T	(p. 235)	9.	F	(p. 242)	16.	T	(p. 246)
3.	F	(p. 221)	10.	T	(p. 232)	17.	F	(pp. 241–242)
4.	F	(p. 238)	11.	T	(p. 246)	18.	F	(p. 224)
5.	F	(p. 229)	12.	T	(p. 223)	19.	F	(p. 232)
6.	T	(p. 238)	13.	T	(p. 222)	20.	F	(p. 246)
7.	T	(p. 246)	14.	F	(pp. 226–227)			

CHAPTER 8

1.	T	(p. 261)	8.	T	(p. 278)	15.	F	(p. 272)
2.	T	(p. 284)	9.	T	(p. 269)	16.	F	(p. 269)
3.	F	(p. 266)	10.	F	(p. 282)	17.	T	(p. 272)
4.	T	(p. 272)	11.	T	(p. 280)	18.	F	(p. 269)
5.	T	(p. 262)	12.	T	(p. 285)	19.	T	(p. 273)
6.	F	(p. 277)	13.	F	(p. 269)	20.	T	(p. 282)
7.	F	(p. 273)	14.	T	(p. 275)			

CHAPTER 9

1.	F	(p. 306)	8.	T	(p. 317)	15.	F	(p. 309)
2.	T	(p. 312)	9.	F	(p. 296)	16.	T	(p. 320)
3.	T	(p. 309)	10.	F	(p. 307)	17.	T	(p. 298)
4.	T	(p. 300)	11.	T	(p. 302)	18.	F	(p. 310)
5.	F	(p. 300)	12.	T	(p. 317)	19.	T	(p. 307)
6.	T	(p. 306)	13.	F	(p. 303)	20.	T	(p. 317)
7.	T	(p. 310)	14.	T	(p. 301)			

CHAPTER 10

1.	F	(pp. 367–368)	8.	F	(p. 368)	15.	T	(p. 339)
2.	F	(p. 342)	9.	T	(p. 335)	16.	F	(p. 335)
3.	T	(p. 354)	10.	T	(p. 359)	17.	T	(p. 355)
4.	F	(p. 360)	11.	F	(p. 366)	18.	F	(p. 359)
5.	T	(p. 346)	12.	T	(p. 342)	19.	F	(p. 363)
6.	T	(p. 355)	13.	F	(p. 336)	20.	F	(p. 363)
7.	T	(p. 341)	14.	F	(p. 339)			

CHAPTER 11

1.	F	(p. 382)	8.	F	(p. 383)	15.	T	(p. 398)
2.	F	(p. 383)	9.	F	(p. 385)	16.	T	(p. 401)
3.	F	(p. 398)	10.	T	(p. 382)	17.	T	(p. 386)
4.	T	(p. 386)	11.	T	(p. 386)	18.	F	(p. 396)
5.	T	(p. 383)	12.	T	(p. 396)	19.	F	(p. 383)
6.	T	(p. 394)	13.	F	(p. 404)	20.	F	(p. 400)
7.	F	(p. 401)	14.	T	(p. 409)			

CHAPTER 12

1.	F	(p. 424)	8.	T	(p. 423)	15.	T	(p. 442)
2.	F	(p. 423)	9.	F	(p. 420)	16.	F	(p. 422)
3.	F	(p. 425)	10.	T	(p. 425)	17.	F	(p. 432)
4.	F	(pp. 437–438)	11.	T	(p. 422)	18.	T	(pp. 437–438)
5.	F	(p. 434)	12.	T	(p. 425)	19.	F	(p. 439)
6.	F	(p. 436)	13.	T	(p. 435)	20.	T	(p. 442)
7.	T	(p. 421)	14.	T	(p. 442)			